D0568169

HOLY DAYS OF ISRAEL

Your Inspirational Guide

RABBI YECHIEL ECKSTEIN

HOLY DAYS OF ISRAEL

Your Inspirational Guide

RABBI YECHIEL ECKSTEIN

INTERNATIONAL FELLOWSHIP OF CHRISTIANS AND JEWS®

Holy Days of Israel: Your Inspirational Guide

Copyright 2011© by the International Fellowship of Christians & Jews, Inc.
All rights reserved.

Unless otherwise noted, all quotations are taken from the *Holy Bible, New International Version*®, NIV®. Copyright © 1973, 1978, 1984, 2011 by Biblica, Inc.™ Used by permission. All rights reserved worldwide.

Cover and interior design by Design Corps, (www.designcorps.us)
Project staff: Art Cooley, Camerin Courtney, John LaRue, Betsy Schmitt

Published by the International Fellowship of Christians & Jews, Inc.
30 North LaSalle Street, Suite 2600, Chicago, IL 60602-3356

ISBN 978-0-9835327-1-2

First printing: 2011

IMAGES CREDITS

Cover:
Western Wall and *Seder Plate* by **Getty Images**. All other images from **iStockphoto**.

Interior:
All images are from **iStockphoto** unless otherwise indicated.

Bible Picture Gallery — pp. 43; 79; 83
Debbi Cooper — p. 33
Dreamstime — p. 77
Flash90 — pp. 29; 45
Getty — p. 93
IFCJ — pp. 15; 67
ISRANET — pp. 85; 100; 115; 119
JDC — p. 107
Sasson Tiram — p. 37

Table of Contents

Pesach

Shavuot

Rosh Hashanah

Yom Kippur

Sukkot

Introduction

"Speak to the Israelites and say to them: 'These are my appointed festivals, the appointed festivals of the LORD, which you are to proclaim as sacred assemblies.'"

— Leviticus 23:2 —

What is it that holds and binds families together? While that question undoubtedly has a multitude of answers depending on our own family experiences, certainly one of those responses is our shared experiences centered around the holidays. The traditions, the special foods, the preparations that go into the celebrations of these annual events help weave the very fabric of our life together as a family.

These special days serve as markers and milestones throughout the year which make up our family history and become the legacy that is passed down from generation to generation. In short, our shared celebrations define who we are as a family.

The same is true for faith families. And for the Jewish people, it is the observances of these "*sacred assemblies*" which define us as a people and go to the very heart of the Jewish understanding of history, God, the soul, and what it means to be a Jew. More than just observances that commemorate historical events, the holy days of Israel are divinely ordained appointments with God that give meaning and purpose to our lives.

Indeed, the Hebrew word for "holiday" used in the *Torah* is *mo'ed,* which means "rendezvous" or "appointed time." Every *mo'ed*, every Jewish holiday, is a meeting of sorts that not only incorporates the dimensions of time and place, but the spiritual dimension of what it means to be the children of God.

The holidays included in *Holy Days of Israel* describe the major festivals in the Jewish year: the Pilgrim Holidays of Passover, *Shavuot* (Pentecost), and *Sukkot* (Feast of the Tabernacles), when Jews in ancient times were required to visit the Temple in Jerusalem to celebrate; and the High Holy Days comprising *Rosh Hashanah* and *Yom Kippur*.

These festivals give meaning and character to

the Jewish year. They attest to the fact that our history is infused with divine purpose. In the Jewish view, events do not occur at random or in isolation from one another, but instead form part of an unfolding divine plan leading to the world's ultimate redemption.

As Abraham J. Karp wrote in his book *The Jewish Way of Life*, "The holidays are the jewels on the crown of Judaism. They add beauty to the life of a people whose vocation is to proclaim the sovereignty of God . . . He [man] desists from labor and soars through heart and mind to spheres of spiritual delight. He breaks the bonds of time as he relives experiences of ages past and envisions with the prophets the end of days." The holidays are spiritual way stations dotting the Jewish calendar, invigorating the Jewish soul, and sanctifying our lives.

Holy Days of Israel is designed to provide you, our Christian friends and supporters of *The Fellowship*, with a deeper and greater understanding of these important milestones and celebrations of the Jewish calendar, and consequently, a better understanding of your own faith.

As you read through each section, I hope you will become more aware of the Jewish roots of the Christian faith and the rituals and traditions that are derived from these observances. The devotions, interspersed between the lessons throughout the book, will help you reflect on the underlying principles and teachings from Scripture that we share as people of faith.

Finally, it is my heartfelt hope that the lessons and devotions included in *Holy Days of Israel* will help you, a treasured member of *The Fellowship* family, discover the beauty and meaning of these divinely ordained "jewels" and lead you to a deeper understanding of your faith and a closer relationship with the God of Israel.

With prayers for *shalom*, peace,

Rabbi Eckstein

HOLY DAYS OF ISRAEL

פֶּסַח

"The LORD said to Moses and Aaron in Egypt, 'This month is to be for you the first month, the first month of your year. Tell the whole community of Israel that on the tenth day of this month each man is to take a lamb for his family, one for each household. . . . That same night they are to eat the meat roasted over the fire, along with bitter herbs, and bread made without yeast. . . . Eat it in haste; it is the LORD's Passover.'"

— EXODUS 12:1–3; 8, 11 —

PASSOVER

the festival of unleavened bread

Passover, or *Pesach* in Hebrew, commemorates the most influential event in Jewish history — the Exodus of the people of Israel from bondage in Egypt. It was at that particular juncture three thousand years ago that the national Jewish identity was shaped, and it was from this event that some of the most profound affirmations of the Jewish faith were drawn.

Primary among them is the notion that God is not some distant power, uninterested in His creation. No, the story of Passover affirms for the Jewish people that God is present in human life, that He hears the cries of His people, and that He intervenes in human history to deliver His people from affliction and redeem us from oppression so we can experience His promises and be in His presence.

A TIME OF DELIVERANCE

God heard their entreaties and called Moses to lead them out of slavery.

One of the key elements of the Passover celebration is retelling the story of the Exodus. In doing so, Jews are to symbolically relive the events and feel as if we were just delivered from Egyptian bondage. Judaism maintains that God's act of liberation is not a one-time-only event, but an ongoing and repeated one. In the words of the *Haggadah*, the text we use during the *Seder* meal to retell the Exodus story, "For God did not redeem our ancestors alone, but us, as well."

The story (found in the Bible from Genesis 37—Exodus 14) begins with Joseph, sold into slavery by his jealous brothers. Joseph ended up in Egypt, where he became the house servant to a good man with a lying wife. Through false accusations, Joseph wound up in jail. But when God allowed him to interpret the dreams of Pharaoh, Egypt's leader, and warn him of a devastating famine ahead, Joseph was appointed the second most powerful leader in all of Egypt.

When the famine came, it impacted Joseph's family back in Israel as well. They went to Egypt seeking food, not knowing Joseph was the leader overseeing the food distribution. Joseph lovingly forgave his brothers, and they and their families moved to Egypt in order to survive the famine. They lived there freely for many years until a new Pharaoh arose who didn't know about Joseph and, in fear of the growing numbers of Israelites among his people, enslaved the Israelites and brought upon them great suffering.

After hundreds of years of this oppression, the Jews cried out to God to save them. God heard their entreaties and called Moses to lead them out of slavery. Though God got Moses's attention in a miraculous way — through a burning bush that was not consumed — and assured him that He would empower Moses for the task at hand, Moses was afraid and reluctant to step into this leadership role.

In His patience and compassion, God told Moses that his brother Aaron could help him, and that God would allow them to perform miracles to show that they were indeed God's appointed spokesmen.

Finally, Moses agreed to be God's servant and obediently went to Pharaoh with God's message: *"Let my people go."*

"WHY, *LORD*, DO YOU STAND FAR OFF? WHY DO YOU HIDE YOURSELF IN TIMES OF TROUBLE?"

—PSALM 10:1

WHERE ARE YOU?

Sometimes it may feel like God is far away. When you are in the midst of a difficult time — whether you're struggling to find a job, or a loved one is losing a battle against cancer, or your child is involved in ungodly activities — it may at times feel like God is nowhere to be found.

"Why do you hide yourself in times of trouble?" At various points in his life, David (the author of this psalm) probably had good reason to question where God was and what He was doing. Where was God when David was running for his life from the jealous King Saul? Where was God when David's own son led an uprising and attempted to take over his father's kingdom? Where was God when David was surrounded by arrogant men who had no room in their hearts for God?

It's at the low points in our lives that God seems to be far away, hiding from us. And it's times like that when we are tempted to let those doubts come between us and God. We may stop praying; we may shut ourselves off from the very One who can carry us through these difficulties. We might look at our circumstances and conclude that God simply does not care.

But notice what David did in this psalm. Despite his doubts, David continued praying and asking God to come quickly to his aid. David didn't

DEVOTION

assume that because of his current situation God did not care or was unwilling to help him. Rather, David affirmed what he knew about God from his past experiences — *"But you, God, see the trouble of the afflicted"* (v. 14). David knew that he was not alone; God knew what was happening, and was with David in his troubles.

The Psalmist David: Worship, by Julius Schnorr von Carolsfeld

This is one of the key messages of Passover: God hears the cries of His people. That is the story of the Exodus. God heard the cries of the Israelites and miraculously delivered them from slavery to freedom.

Thankfully, He is the same compassionate and listening God for us today. It is the times when we are alone, when we feel abandoned and oppressed, that we most need to remember that truth and pray to God. Tell Him your troubles. Share with Him your doubts. Cry out for His help. Then hold on to the truth, knowing, as the Israelites and King David did, that *"You, LORD, hear the desire of the afflicted; you encourage them, and you listen to their cry"* (v. 17).

GOING DEEPER FOR CHRISTIANS

For a Christian perspective on answered prayers, read these Scriptures:

- Mark 11:23–25
- 2 Corinthians 1:10–11
- Philippians 4:5–7
- James 5:14–16
- 1 John 5:13–15

... so that we may never again forget God's power and His mercy.

Battle of the Gods

One of the key players in the drama of the Exodus story was Pharaoh, the Egyptian king. Even before Moses and Aaron appeared before him, they were well aware of the difficult task ahead of them. God had forewarned them that Pharaoh would not easily let the Israelites leave.

In fact, God told Moses and Aaron that Pharaoh would *"harden his heart"* and refuse to let God's people go despite the plagues and disasters that would be brought upon the land and the people. Unmoved by the miracles Moses and Aaron performed in his presence, Pharaoh refused their request to release the Israelites. After all, his magicians were also able to perform the same miracles.

It gets harder, however, to understand his continued refusal when God allowed Moses to turn the Nile River into blood — and when plagues of frogs, gnats, flies, illness, boils, hail, locusts, and darkness descended on his kingdom. Despite all these displays of God's power, Pharaoh's heart was hardened, and he refused to release the Israelites. In many ways, God was exceedingly patient with Pharaoh.

Initially, the Bible records that Pharaoh hardened his own heart

(Exodus 7:13, *"became hard"*; v. 14, *"unyielding"*; v. 22, *"became hard"*). Pharaoh hardened his own heart six times by refusing Moses's requests. Then, after the seventh plague, God is said to have hardened Pharaoh's heart — and by doing so, confirmed the Egyptian king's willful disobedience and stubbornness.

Since Pharaoh's heart remained callous and stubborn, it was ultimately necessary for the tenth and final plague, the death of all firstborn sons throughout the land of Egypt.

Incredibly, Moses had warned Pharaoh that this would happen if he did not obey God. (See Exodus 4:21–23.) And in that first *Pesach*, meaning Passover, God proved to Pharaoh and all Egypt who was supreme and all-powerful.

The *Torah* tells Jews to mark this entire series of events — from the bitterness of slavery by the Egyptians to the plague of death passing over the homes marked by lamb's blood — by celebrating the *Pesach* festival and recalling our salvation from Egyptian oppression, so that we may never again forget God's power and His mercy.

"BUT THE EGYPTIAN MAGICIANS DID THE SAME THINGS BY THEIR SECRET ARTS, AND PHARAOH'S HEART BECAME HARD; HE WOULD NOT LISTEN TO MOSES AND AARON, JUST AS THE LORD HAD SAID."

—EXODUS 7:22

A HARDENED HEART

No matter what one's age, it's wise to make a yearly visit to our doctors for a complete physical. That way we check our cholesterol, weight, blood pressure, and other key indicators to get a picture of our overall health. Depending on the results, we then can make the necessary changes to improve our physical well-being.

Undergoing routine checkups is a great idea for anything you want to keep in good condition — your health, your teeth, even your car! But what about your spiritual health? When was the last time you checked the condition of your heart, spiritually speaking?

From the story of the Exodus, we can see what happens when our heart becomes hard. Initially Pharaoh had hardened his heart, but as his stubbornness and disobedience continued, God allowed Pharaoh's heart to remain obstinate and recalcitrant.

While it is easy to judge Pharaoh for his hard and stubborn heart, we must be careful to attend to the condition of our own hearts. A hardened heart doesn't happen all at once. It results from stubbornly and consistently setting ourselves against God, just as Pharaoh did. In choosing to disregard God's will and

DEVOTION

command, we can become so hardened that we no longer are able to listen to Him and we can no longer turn to Him for forgiveness.

Certainly, many will experience times of rebellion and stubbornness. But we can keep our hearts soft and open to God through prayer and worship. In Hebrew, "to pray" means "to judge oneself." True prayer always must involve introspection, meditation, and self-scrutiny. As we do this and continually bring our confession and sins before God, we will lessen our chances of becoming hardhearted.

Take a few moments this week for a spiritual heart-check. In what areas of your life do you find yourself resisting God's call? Where is He prompting you to turn toward Him? God wants to soften your heart today.

Moses and Aaron Before Pharaoh, by Gustave Doré

Going Deeper for Christians

For a Christian perspective on your spiritual condition, read these Scriptures:

- 2 Corinthians 5:17
- Galatians 6:15
- Ephesians 2:1–5
- 1 Peter 4:1–6

Matzah, "poor man's bread," reminds Jews to be humble and never forget our former life of servitude.

Foods Rich with Meaning

Passover is also called the Festival of Unleavened Bread because of the major role *matzah* plays in the remembrance and the celebration of the Exodus story. Since the Jews were in such a hurry to leave Egypt when Pharaoh finally let them go, there was no time to allow the dough to rise for the bread baking that day. So they took the dough with them and then made it into a hard flatbread, or *matzah*, over their open fires in the desert.

Some rabbis have taught that *matzah* is so significant to Passover because it symbolizes the fact that the people of Israel had such deep, abiding trust in God that they were willing even to leave the security and comfort of their homes in Egypt and to enter into the dry, barren desert. Others teach that because *matzah* is considered "poor man's bread," it reminds Jews to be humble and to never forget our former life of servitude. By remembering this difficult past, Jews are all the more grateful for the freedom God miraculously secured for us.

Matzah is one of the key foods eaten during *Seder*, the special meal to commemorate the Exodus. And it's not the only food at the meal rife with spiritual meaning. Here are a few of the other foods included:

The ***Afikomen*** is the "dessert," or the piece of *matzah* hidden during the service and sought out by children toward the end of the meal. It symbolizes the Passover lamb, which was eaten at the end of the meal.

Wine (or grape juice) plays a big part in the *Seder*. It is traditional to drink four glasses of wine during the *Seder* to symbolize the Jewish people's trust in God's **fourfold promise** of redemption:

"I am the Lord, and ***I will bring you out*** *from under the yoke of the Egyptians.* ***I will free you from being slaves*** *to them, and* ***I will redeem you*** *with an outstretched arm and with mighty acts of judgment. I will take you as my own people, and* ***I will be your God****."* —Exodus 6:6–7, emphasis added

Elijah's Cup is a fifth glass of wine, filled only at the conclusion of the *Seder*, and it represents the fifth stage of God's promise of redemption: *"And I will bring you to the land I swore with uplifted hand to give to Abraham, to Isaac and to Jacob"* (Exodus 6:8).

According to Jewish tradition, the fifth glass is poured but not drunk symbolizing that God's promise for the Jewish people's return to our homeland remains unfulfilled. It is called Elijah's Cup since, according to tradition, it is the prophet Elijah who will usher in the Messiah and the ingathering of the Jewish people into Israel.

"FOR SEVEN DAYS YOU ARE TO EAT BREAD MADE WITHOUT YEAST. ON THE FIRST DAY REMOVE THE YEAST FROM YOUR HOUSES, FOR WHOEVER EATS ANYTHING WITH YEAST IN IT FROM THE FIRST DAY THROUGH THE SEVENTH MUST BE CUT OFF FROM ISRAEL."

—EXODUS 12:15

SPRING CLEANING

Maybe yours is one of those households that undergoes a thorough and careful spring cleaning, where every nook and cranny in the house gets a good scrubbing, and where every closet and drawer gets a painstaking purge of all unwanted and used items. While a lot of hard work and effort goes into it, afterward we feel our load lightened a bit; we feel refreshed and renewed.

During the Passover celebration, Jews undergo a similar exercise of meticulous and painstaking cleaning as part of our observance. During that first Passover, God commanded the Israelites not only to eat unleavened bread for seven days, but they also had to remove any trace of yeast from their homes. To do otherwise would result in that person being cut off from the rest of the community.

It is a command that Jews take very seriously. Prior to the holiday, we meticulously clean our houses, searching for any traces of yeast, or *chametz*, as it is called in Hebrew. We set aside certain utensils for Passover, which never come into contact with *chametz*. On the evening before Passover, we conduct the *bedikat chametz*, or "searching for leaven," ceremony, in which

DEVOTION

the family goes through the entire house with a candle searching for any leaven that might have been overlooked.

Chametz can be understood in two different ways. While it certainly refers to the physical removal of leavened products from the household, it also is used to suggest a spiritual contamination. Spiritual *chametz* consists of those wrong actions and unhealthy thoughts that damage our lives. Before Passover, we make an effort to get rid of our spiritual *chametz* as well as the physical *chametz* in our lives so that we can begin the spring with a clean slate.

As we enter into this time of celebration of both Passover and, for Christians, Easter, let us remember our need to clean house spiritually. Take some time during this week to search the corners of your soul for any *chametz* so your relationship with God and with others is open and fulfilling.

GOING DEEPER FOR CHRISTIANS

For a Christian perspective on your need for spiritual cleansing, read these Scriptures:

- Romans 12:2
- Ephesians 4:31–32
- Colossians 3:8–10
- Hebrews 10:22

Passover bids us to affirm the indissoluble link between slavery and redemption, between our tribulations and our joys.

A Holy Meal

The *Seder* meal is the centerpiece of the Passover celebration. While many Jewish holidays revolve around the synagogue, the *Seder* customarily takes place at home. Key to the meal is the *Seder* plate, which contains six unique foods that symbolize the experience of the Jewish people as they moved from bondage and slavery in Egypt to freedom as God's chosen people. These *Seder* foods include:

Charoset is a mixture of apples, nuts, and red wine or grape juice. This mixture symbolizes the mortar the Jewish slaves made in the building of cities of Egypt for Pharaoh and his kingdom.

Zeroa is a roasted shank bone of lamb or neck of a chicken, representing the paschal lamb that was sacrificed and eaten at Passover during the time when the Temple was the central place of worship for the Jewish people.

Maror and ***Chazeret*** are two bitter herbs, often horseradish and romaine lettuce, that represent the bitterness of life under slavery.

Baytza is an egg that is first hard-boiled, then roasted, serving as a reminder of the festival sacrifice during the time of the Temple. With its destruction, the Jews began to associate the egg with the loss of the Temple. Today the egg is a reminder for us to mourn the suffering of all people living under bondage and slavery.

Karpas is a green vegetable, usually parsley or celery, which represents the reemergence of life at springtime. During the *Seder*, the *karpas* is dipped in salt water and eaten. The salt water represents the tears of suffering that became tears of joy as the people moved from slavery to freedom.

Passover bids us to affirm the indissoluble link between slavery and redemption, between our tribulations and our joys. To lose sight of either, or of the tension that affirming both necessarily involves, is to miss the mark. We are neither to be fixated and obsessed with past suffering nor overly and unrealistically optimistic about the future. For this reason, explain the rabbis, we begin the *Seder* with deprecating remarks of how our ancestors were once slaves in Egypt, but conclude it by praising God for delivering us from our suffering.

"ON THAT DAY TELL YOUR SON, 'I DO THIS BECAUSE OF WHAT THE LORD DID FOR ME WHEN I CAME OUT OF EGYPT.' THIS OBSERVANCE WILL BE FOR YOU LIKE A SIGN ON YOUR HAND AND A REMINDER ON YOUR FOREHEAD THAT THIS LAW OF THE LORD IS TO BE ON YOUR LIPS. FOR THE LORD BROUGHT YOU OUT OF EGYPT WITH HIS MIGHTY HAND."

—EXODUS 13:8–9

A MEAL TO REMEMBER

How do you share with your family the important events and traditions that you hold dear? Maybe on certain anniversaries, you visit the place where you grew up. Or perhaps you spend time with your children looking through old photos and recounting the stories behind them. Maybe your family holds yearly reunions where the entire clan gathers and shares memories.

Whatever you might do, you know it's important to understand your roots and to celebrate the traditions and history that make your family unique.

That's true for faith families, as well. During our Passover celebration, Jews share our roots, our traditions, our history, and our faith through the *Seder* meal. It not only helps us *tell* the story, but it also helps us to *reenact* the events as if we were there.

The story of the Exodus from Egypt has been a spiritual inspiration for people all over the world. Over the centuries, the liturgy of the *Haggadah*, the guide to the *Seder*, was developed to include the strivings for freedom of Jews who had no homeland. Even today, Jews

DEVOTION

who feel distanced from the mainstream Jewish community continue to create liturgy for Passover that expresses their wish for freedom and redemption from a sense of isolation.

Observance of the Passover binds us throughout history with those first Israelites who came out of bondage from Egypt. And it marks us as unique followers of God.

What about you? What in your faith traditions mark you as a person of faith and a follower of God? What do you do that sets you apart? Perhaps it is the way you raise your children, or care for the poor, or demonstrate love for others that marks you as different.

Whatever it might be, think of how you can be a blessing to others, then celebrate that within your own family, and pass it along to the next generation.

The First Passover, by Julius Schnorr von Carolsfeld

GOING DEEPER FOR CHRISTIANS

For a Christian perspective on expressing your faith, read these Scriptures:

- Matthew 28:18–20
- Mark 5:18–20
- Acts 1:8

True freedom and redemption, in the Jewish view, involves both spiritual and physical liberation.

Spiritual Freedom

Freedom, both in the spiritual and physical sense, is an underlying theme of the Passover celebration. One of the many ways we express this idea of freedom during the *Seder* meal, in particular, is how we sit. As we drink the wine throughout *Seder*, we recline slightly, as was the manner of Roman emperors, to demonstrate our freedom on this day.

Even if we live under conditions of oppression and are not, in fact, physically free, we are to *feel* as if we are. *Pesach* reminds us that true freedom also involves the inner, spiritual realm. It cannot be externally denied, nor can a condition of slavery and servitude be outwardly imposed. The physically oppressed must also recline and feel like emperors on *Pesach* night. According to the *Talmud*, those who are poor must even sell their clothes or borrow money if necessary to buy wine for the four cups! Nothing must stand in the way of fulfilling the *mitzvah* (spiritual duty) of feeling free on this holiday.

In addition to recalling our Exodus from Egypt long ago, Jews are also urged to actively pursue freedom for all those to whom it is presently denied. That is the meaning of the biblical command to love the strangers in our midst since we were once strangers in Egypt, and we can best understand their hearts. And while bringing about man's spiritual freedom and redemption is, of course, a significant part of the Jewish mission, Judaism regards the poor, the hungry, and the oppressed as equally enslaved and also in need of redemption, albeit of a materialistic kind.

True freedom and redemption, in the Jewish view, involves both spiritual and physical liberation. And Jews are commanded to take an active part in extending this freedom to all people.

"When a foreigner resides among you in your land, do not mistreat them. The foreigner residing among you must be treated as your native-born. Love them as yourself, for you were foreigners in Egypt. I am the Lord your God."

—Leviticus 19:33–34

The Festival of Freedom

In retelling the story of the Exodus, perhaps that hardest thing for many of us to connect with is the concept of being an enslaved people. Living in the United States, or even Israel for that matter, we enjoy freedom to worship, freedom to pursue a career or education, freedom to speak, and freedom to elect our government. We are, by the world's standards, a free people.

Yet, Passover reminds us that true freedom also involves the inner, spiritual realm. It is true that in a time of freedom we can feel enslaved. And it is equally true that while enslaved or under oppression, we can feel free.

We marvel at how it was humanly possible for Jews living in concentration camps and the Warsaw Ghetto during the Holocaust to fulfill this sense of "feeling free" on Passover. And yet, the amazing testimony to the power of God's spirit moving within humankind is that many Jews *did* find the spiritual strength and courage to feel free despite their wretched conditions.

Passover bids us to remember the good and the bad, our joys and

DEVOTION

our tribulations, our past sufferings and our hopes for the world's future redemption. In recalling our own Exodus from slavery and bondage, we are to actively seek freedom for all those to whom it is presently denied — whether it's spiritual freedom, or freedom from such things as hunger or poverty.

The very essence of Passover and our longing for freedom — both physical and spiritual — is expressed beautifully in the closing reading of the *Seder* liturgy:

> "Our Passover service is completed. We have reverently repeated its ordered traditions. With songs of praise we have called upon the name of God. May he who broke Pharaoh's yoke forever shatter all fetters of oppression, and hasten the day when war will be no more. Soon may he bring redemption to all mankind — freed from violence and from wrong, and united in an eternal covenant of brotherhood."

That is a hope and prayer that Christians and Jews can share.

GOING DEEPER FOR CHRISTIANS

For a Christian perspective on freedom, read these Scriptures:

- Luke 4:18–19
- Romans 8:20–22
- 2 Corinthians 3:17
- Galatians 4:3–7; 5:1
- 1 Peter 2:16

The *Korban Pesach* — Passover lamb — was a tangible reminder to the people of their special relationship to God.

THE PASSOVER LAMB

Many of the sacred aspects of Christian worship trace their spiritual roots directly to the Jewish faith and the early history of the nation of Israel. Such is the case with the term "Paschal Lamb" or "Lamb of God," which in the Christian tradition refers to Jesus. In the Jewish faith, the term is *Korban Pesach*, or "sacrifice of Passover," which dates back to the Exodus from Egypt.

In the times of the Jewish Temple worship — both in Solomon's Temple and the Second Temple — Jews obeyed God's command to remember that first Passover by sacrificing a lamb on that day. The lamb had to be male, one year old, and, most importantly, without blemish. (See Exodus 12:5.) Only then would it suffice to be the perfect Passover sacrifice.

This Passover observance is what the Christians Scriptures reference when speaking of *"a lamb without blemish or defect"* (1 Peter 1:19) — referring to the sacrificial death of Jesus.

The word *korban,* "sacrifice," is related to *le-karev*, which means to come close. Through the sacrifice, worshippers felt they were giving themselves vicariously to God. In addition, these offerings required a great sacrifice on the part of the people. They were, in fact, giving up something from their prized possessions since the required sacrifice was to come from their own flock. In making this sacrifice in connection with the Temple rites, the people were giving up a precious source of income and food.

The *Korban Pesach* was a tangible reminder to the people of their special relationship to God and His mercy in rescuing and saving them from the plague of death. In protecting them from this tenth plague, God made the Jewish people His personal nation, and they therefore earned the privilege of serving Him. By performing this sacrifice each year at Passover, the people were acknowledging the unique relationship they had with God.

This quality is still a feature of the Jewish people today. There has never been a successful attempt by Jews to integrate into any other nation; we have always remained distinct, a people apart.

"GIVE THANKS TO THE LORD, FOR HE IS GOOD; HIS LOVE ENDURES FOREVER. LET THE REDEEMED OF THE LORD TELL THEIR STORY — THOSE HE REDEEMED FROM THE HAND OF THE FOE."

—PSALM 107:1–2

OUR GOD WHO RESCUES

Some may remember watching the televised events as hundreds worked around the clock to rescue thirty-three Chilean miners who had been trapped underground for sixty-eight days. More than a billion people watched as that first miner emerged and stepped before a throng of cheering family and other concerned observers.

It was an emotional moment for anyone watching this remarkable rescue, and indeed, as one observer wrote later, "They became an example to the world, a symbol of survival. A brief reminder that like evil, good exists. And a reminder that in an ever more connected world, a single event has the power to unite us."

Great and amazing stories of rescues have the power to unite and encourage us. Throughout the Bible, we encounter a God who delights in rescuing His people. He rescued righteous Noah and his family from the punishing flood. He rescued Jonah from the belly of a whale. God used Esther to rescue the Jews from the evil Haman. Time and again God rescued the Jews from attacking armies. And at that first Passover, God rescued the Israelites out of slavery in Egypt.

Psalm 107 celebrates God's gracious habit of rescuing His people. The opening verses are a call to praise God for His redeeming work. The

DEVOTION

psalm writer explores the depths of God's goodness by portraying four distinct ways that God reaches down to rescue those who trust in Him: the wanderers (107:4–9); the prisoners (107:10–16); the distressed (107:17–20); and the storm-tossed (107:23–30).

Today, when we are rarely in physical danger and seldom in need of the type of rescue we read about so often in the Bible, it's sometimes difficult to remember that our God is a God who rescues. But the God we love and serve today is the same God who saved Noah, Jonah, David, and the Israelites. And this is a good thing, because we still need rescuing, even if only — or perhaps most importantly — from ourselves and our sinful ways.

We who seek to follow God today must be as hungry and thirsty for His holy word and His blessing as were the people described in Psalm 107. At times, we too may feel like weary travelers, prisoners in chains, the sick or distressed, or storm-tossed sailors. But God can reach down and bring us out of any circumstance if we will put our hope and trust in Him.

Let's give thanks to God today for His goodness and trust that because of His love for us, He will rescue us in our time of need.

GOING DEEPER FOR CHRISTIANS

For a Christian perspective on God's ability to rescue you, read these Scriptures:

- Matthew 16:24–26
- Mark 16:15–16
- Luke 19:10
- John 3:16–17
- Romans 5:9–11
- Galatians 1:3–5
- Colossians 1:13–14

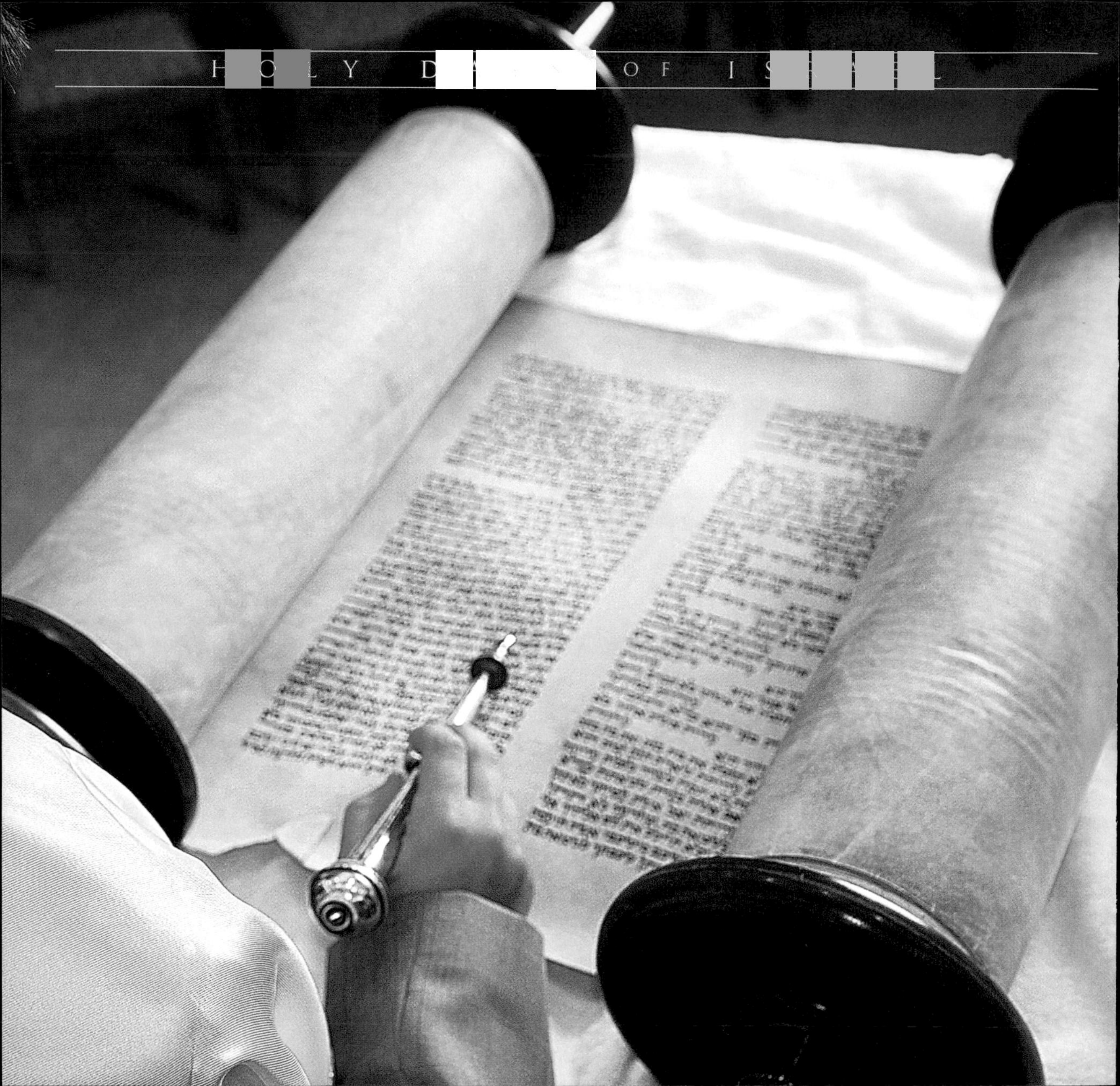

שָׁבוּעוֹת

"From the day after the Sabbath . . . count off seven full weeks. Count off fifty days up to the day after the seventh Sabbath, and then present an offering of new grain to the LORD."

— LEVITICUS 23:15–16 —

SHAVUOT

the feast of weeks

The Jewish festival of *Shavuot* has dual significance. First, it commemorates the ancient obligation to bring the harvest's "first fruits" to the Holy Temple in Jerusalem as an offering to God. Second, it commemorates an event of monumental significance to both Christians and Jews alike — the giving of the *Torah*, the first five books of what Christians call the Old Testament, on Mount Sinai.

Shavuot falls fifty days after Passover, and the holidays are linked by more than their proximity. The Exodus from Egypt, which Passover celebrates, marked the beginning of *physical* freedom for the Jewish people. But *Shavuot* reminds us that physical liberation was incomplete without the *spiritual* redemption represented by receiving God's law. The Jewish people did not leave Egypt for simple autonomy: They left slavery to Pharaoh in order to become servants of God. True freedom is not just an absence of physical bondage, but is an action: voluntary servitude to God.

The people would bring their first fruits to the Temple amid great pomp and ceremony.

A SACRED ANNIVERSARY

Shavuot, or the Feast of Weeks, is a Jewish holiday that commemorates the single most important event in Israel's history: the giving of the *Torah* to Moses at Mount Sinai. Although it is not as well known among non-Jews as Passover or *Sukkot* (the Feast of Booths), it is one of the three major God-ordained festivals often called "pilgrim" festivals because all Jewish males were required to observe them at the Holy Temple in Jerusalem.

More than three thousand years ago, after leaving Egypt on the night of Passover, the Jews traveled to the Sinai Desert. During that journey, they experienced divine revelation as God gave the Jewish people His law. In Deuteronomy 4:10–13, Moses reminded the people of that experience:

"Remember the day you stood before the LORD your God at Horeb [Sinai]. . . . You came near and stood at the foot of the mountain while it blazed with fire to the very heavens, with black clouds and deep darkness. Then the LORD spoke. . . . He declared to you his covenant, the Ten Commandments, which he commanded you to follow and then wrote them on two stone tablets."

Shavuot is the culmination of the seven weeks between Passover and the giving of the law. Indeed, the very term *Shavuot* means "weeks." Since *Shavuot* occurs fifty days after the first day of Passover, it is sometimes known as Pentecost, which is a Greek word that means "fifty." Jesus's followers were in Jerusalem celebrating Pentecost when, according to the Christian tradition, the Holy Spirit was given to them, so many Christians today celebrate Pentecost as the birth of the church.

Shavuot is also called *Atzeret*, meaning "the completion," because together with Passover it forms the completion of a unit. Jews gained their freedom from Egypt on Passover in order to receive the *Torah* on *Shavuot*.

The earlier celebrations of *Shavuot* were more agricultural in nature and motif. In ancient times, sheaves of barley (the winter crop) were brought to the Temple each day, starting on Passover until *Shavuot*, which is the beginning of the harvest season fifty days later. Farmers looked forward to *Shavuot* with great anticipation. When it finally arrived, the people would bring their first fruits to the Temple amid great pomp and ceremony. They rejoiced before God and thanked Him for their material blessings.

"GIVE ME UNDERSTANDING, SO THAT I MAY KEEP YOUR LAW AND OBEY IT WITH ALL MY HEART. DIRECT ME IN THE PATH OF YOUR COMMANDS, FOR THERE I FIND DELIGHT."
—PSALM 119:34–35

CELEBRATING THE WORD

We celebrate many significant different things — job promotions, engagements, birthdays, anniversaries, graduations. But what about God's word? Have you ever stopped to celebrate the fact that you can read, study, meditate, and grow spiritually from reading God's word?

During *Shavuot*, Jews in Israel and throughout the world do just that. According to calculations based on Exodus 19:1, this was the very day that the Jews came to the foot of Mount Sinai, where they received the *Torah*, the first five books of the Hebrew Bible.

Just as a groom longingly awaits the time when he can be with his bride, so, explain the Jewish mystics, we count the days until we can greet our beloved — the *Torah*. In counting the days between Passover and *Shavuot*, Jews declare that man does not attain complete freedom through physical liberation alone.

The Exodus of God's people from Egypt was not complete without a spiritual redemption. That was achieved when the Israelites received God's law, and thus, were born as God's people, whose ultimate purpose was to serve Him. Indeed, Moses declared to Pharaoh: *"Let my people go, so that they*

DEVOTION

may serve me" (Exodus 9:13, ESV). In the Jewish view, true freedom is servitude to God.

Rabbinical literature also states, "A truly free man is one who engages in the study and practice of *Torah*." Therefore, many Jews celebrate that on *Shavuot* by staying up the entire night studying the *Torah*. Jewish children even stay up late and eat candy as a reminder that the *Torah* is sweet.

Perhaps during this week, you may consider how you can honor God's word, as well. Maybe pick one of your favorite verses and memorize it. Or use today's Scriptures. God's word is worthy of celebration!

Ezra Reading the Law, by Julius Schnorr von Carolsfeld

GOING DEEPER FOR CHRISTIANS

For a Christian perspective on God's word, read these Scriptures:

- Matthew 4:4; 13:18–23
- Mark 13:31
- John 1:1; 5:24
- Hebrews 4:12

We are to strive for spiritual growth year-round.

A Spiritual Shift

With the destruction of the Second Temple and the forced separation of the Jewish people from their land, the centrality of the harvest motif on *Shavuot* diminished. Instead, the theme of the anniversary of the revelation of the *Torah* to Moses on Mount Sinai gained dominance — a theme that has continued today.

At synagogue services on *Shavuot* morning, the divinely communicated Ten Commandments are read, and Jews reaffirm their commitment to treasure and obey God's law.

According to a well-known Jewish *Midrash* (the oral traditions that eventually were written down), God initially offered the *Torah* to each of seventy nations, who would not accept it without first asking what it was about. After hearing the commandments, each nation had some excuse for not accepting them. God finally turned to the nation of Israel, who said, *"Kol asher diber Ad-onai na'aseh,"* which means "all that the LORD says we will do." Unlike the other nations, Israel chose the *Torah* before knowing its contents (Exodus 19:8).

Today, during the morning service on *Shavuot*, Jews reaffirm our commitment to God, to the *Torah*, and to our faith, by repeating those same words: "All that the LORD says we will do."

Additionally, *Shavuot* reminds us that we are to strive for spiritual growth year-round. Why, ask the Hasidic rabbis, is the holiday referred to as "the season of the *giving* of *Torah*" instead of as "the season of our *receiving* of the *Torah*"? They argue that although it was given to our forefathers at Sinai on that specific date, we are to receive it everywhere, on all occasions.

"So Moses went back and summoned the elders of the people and set before them all the words the Lord had commanded him to speak. The people all responded together, 'We will do everything the Lord has said.'"
—Exodus 19:7–8

Renewing Our Vows

One of the most anticipated stops on *The Fellowship*'s *Journey Home Tour* to Israel is a visit to the church at Cana, where Jesus performed his first miracle: turning water into wine at a marriage celebration. It's here that couples on the tour can renew their marriage vows — and many choose to do so!

It's always a moving ceremony to see couples of all ages come forward and recommit themselves to one another. It's a wonderful reminder of our need to revisit and renew those bonds and commitments which are most precious to us. It's in this spirit that Jews recommit ourselves to obeying and honoring God's law during the celebration of *Shavuot*.

We also read from the book of Ruth during that service, not only because of its link to the harvest season (when the story takes place), but also because of Ruth's beautiful vow of acceptance of the Jewish faith and God: *"Where you go I will go, and where you stay I will stay. Your people will be my people and your God my God"* (Ruth 1:16).

Although foreign-born, Ruth was willing to leave her home, her family, and her country and travel with her mother-in-law Naomi to Israel because

DEVOTION

of her deep love for God and the *Torah*. And God blessed her greatly by giving her a son. Through this son, she would be eternally grafted into the family line that produced King David, and from this family line would one day come the Messiah.

Let us also affirm and renew our commitment to God and to obeying His word, just as Ruth did thousands of years ago.

Ruth and Naomi Leaving Moab, by Julius Schnorr von Carolsfeld

Going Deeper for Christians

For a Christian perspective on renewing your commitment to follow God, read these Scriptures:

- Matthew 16:13–16
- Romans 10:9–10
- 1 Timothy 6:12
- 2 Timothy 2:19
- Hebrews 13:15

The *Torah* is the very lifeblood of the Jewish people.

Significance of the *Torah*

To understand the significance of *Shavuot*, one must also understand the significance of the *Torah* in the life of the Jew. It is not just a text given to Moses at Sinai that Jews celebrate this day. The *Torah* guides the Jew's path, shapes his character, and links him with the divine. The *Torah* is the lens through which the Jew perceives life and reality; it is that which unites him with his fellow Jew. The *Torah* is the very lifeblood of the Jewish people.

The term *Torah* is generally used in reference to the Bible that Jews refer to as the *Tanakh* and Christians refer to as the Hebrew Bible or Old Testament. In its narrowest sense, the term *Torah* refers to the five books of Moses, or the *Pentateuch*.

The traditional view of the *Torah* is that it is the embodiment of God's word, the essential means of knowing God and His divine will for man. Although given to the people of Israel at a particular juncture in history, it is, nevertheless, eternally valid and authoritative. Everything there is to know about life, claim the rabbis, can be derived from the *Torah*. As the Psalmist declared, *"The law [Torah] of the Lord is perfect, refreshing the soul"* (Psalm 19:7).

The *Torah* is written on parchment and tied together in a scroll. It is the holiest ritual object in Judaism in that it contains both the name and message of God. The *Torah* is to be treated with utmost reverence and respect. It may not be desecrated or defiled. Indeed, there are numerous laws pertaining to the sanctity with which we are to treat the *Torah*.

There are many theories about how God revealed His word through the *Torah* — that He "dictated" it verbatim to Moses on Sinai, that Moses was "inspired" to write it down, that it was all written by man and then sanctioned retroactively by God.

In whatever way people understand the mechanics of the Sinai revelation, they all regard the *Torah* as we have it today as the primary source of our knowledge of God's word to man, and indeed, of God Himself.

It is, in the words of the Jewish liturgy, "given to the children of Israel from the mouth of God through the hand of Moses." And it is this divine act that we celebrate at *Shavuot*.

The Perfect Refreshment

"The law of the Lord is perfect, refreshing the soul."
—Psalm 19:7

How do you refresh yourself? For some of us, it's taking a brisk walk outdoors. Others might find refreshment listening to music or watching TV. Still others might be revitalized by a quick nap, or a long, soothing bath. But what about reading God's word?

That's what refreshed King David! God's law refreshed David's soul. It prepared him for each day. It energized him and enabled him to deal with his circumstances. It made him wise and gave him insight. More than that, it brought him joy.

Consider how David describes God's laws and commands in Psalm 19: God's laws are perfect and make us wise (v. 7); His commandments are right and bring joy to our hearts (v. 8); His word provides us with insight (v. 8) and warns us against bad decisions and foolish living (v. 11). Ultimately, there is a reward for obeying God's word (v. 11).

When David wrote these words, he probably only had the *Torah*, the first five books of the Bible, to read and study. Those books were precious to him, *"more precious than gold"* and *"sweeter than honey"* (v. 10). From those books, David was able to discern what was right and wrong. He had

DEVOTION

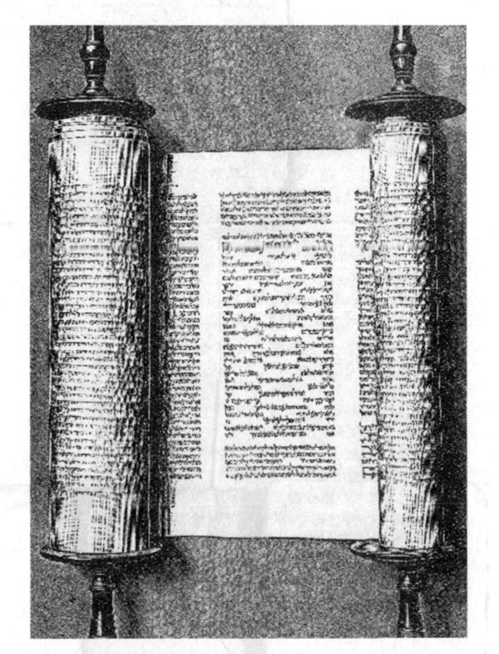

insight into his hidden faults and sinful ways (v. 12). For David, there was no better pastime, no other way to revitalize and refresh himself each day, than to spend time reading and meditating on God's word.

Think of how much richer we are than even King David! For not only do we have the law (the *Torah* for the Jew), but we also have the Psalms, the books of wisdom, and the wonderful stories of the heroes, the prophets, and the people of the Hebrew Bible to inspire us, guide us, warn us, and encourage us.

Consider what you can do in opening up your Bible so that you, like David, will be refreshed and find joy in God's holy and perfect word.

GOING DEEPER FOR CHRISTIANS

For a Christian perspective on refreshing the soul, read these Scriptures:

- Acts 3:19–20
- Romans 15:4
- 2 Thessalonians 2:16–17
- 2 Timothy 3:16

Shavuot was a time for the people to remember all that God had provided for them.

Celebrating the First Fruits

When the people of Israel began to settle into the Promised Land, the celebration of *Shavuot* became an agricultural holiday that celebrated God's provision for His people. In Deuteronomy (the final book of the *Torah*), Moses reminded the people to faithfully celebrate Passover (Deuteronomy 16:1–7), Unleavened Bread (Deuteronomy 16:8), and *Shavuot* (Deuteronomy 16:9–11):

> *"Count off seven weeks from the time you begin to put the sickle to the standing grain. Then celebrate the Festival of Weeks to the LORD your God by giving a freewill offering in proportion to the blessings the LORD your God has given you. And rejoice before the LORD your God at the place he will choose as a dwelling for his Name — you, your sons and daughters, your male and female servants, the Levites in your towns, and the foreigners, the fatherless and the widows living among you."*— Deuteronomy 16:9–11

The Hebrew word *sheva* means "seven," *shavu'ah* means "week," and *Shavuot* means "weeks." So the celebration of *Shavuot* is exactly seven weeks after the first harvest of barley. As one of the three pilgrimage holidays, the people of Israel were to come to the Temple to present the first fruits of their harvest before God.

The first fruits were called *bikkurim*, and referred especially to the seven fruits of the Promised Land — wheat, barley, olives, figs, pomegranates, dates, and grapes (Deuteronomy 8:8). As soon as the farmer saw evidence of a ripening fruit, he would tie a string or ribbon around it and designate that first fruit as *bikkurim*. Later, he would return to pick that fruit, put it in a basket (wicker for the poor or one woven with strands of gold and silver for the more well-to-do), and bring it to the Temple.

At the Temple, each family would present their basket of fruits to the priest and repeat the verses from Deuteronomy 26:5–11: *"Now I bring the firstfruits of the soil that you, Lord, have given me"* (Deuteronomy 26:10).

Shavuot was a time of great rejoicing and celebration. It was a time for the people to remember all that God had provided for them in the Promised Land, and it was a time to express joy and thanksgiving to God.

"The Lord said to Moses, 'Speak to the Israelites and say to them: "When you enter the land I am going to give you and you reap its harvest, bring to the priest a sheaf of the first grain you harvest."'"

—Leviticus 23:9–10

Giving Our Best

When a guest comes to dinner, do you reheat the leftovers from last night's meal? Do you set the table with plastic forks and knives and use soiled placemats? Of course not! Typically, we bring out the best for our guests — the china, silverware, freshly prepared food — right?

Or when it comes to making an important presentation at work, do you scribble a few notes on some scrap paper and draw a pie chart free hand with markers? Of course not! You spend the necessary time to make a professional presentation that is printed ahead of time. In other words, you give it your very best effort.

Giving our best, whether it has to do with serving guests, doing our job, or spending time with our family, is important to us. But what about when it comes to God? Do we give to Him what the Bible refers to as the "first fruits" of our time, our devotion, our labors?

The holiday, *Shavuot*, was originally intended as a celebration of the summer harvest season, a time to thank God for His abundant provision by bringing to Him the first fruits of the harvest. After the Temple was destroyed, the holiday focused more on celebrating the giving of God's law.

DEVOTION

The first fruits did not necessarily mean the earliest crop; the term "first fruits" also referred to the best of the crop. As the Bible commanded in Exodus 23.19, *"Bring the best of the firstfruits of your soil to the house of the LORD your God."*

So how do we give God our first fruits? We do that as we live wholly to please Him instead of ourselves. And as we *first* give to Him — our time, hearts, and efforts — we will be blessed.

The Basket of First Fruits

GOING DEEPER FOR CHRISTIANS

For a Christian perspective on doing your best, read these Scriptures:

- Mark 12:33
- Philippians 4:8
- Colossians 3:17
- 2 Timothy 2:15

The *Akdamot* glorifies God for creating the world and for choosing Israel as His special people.

A Celebration of God's Gifts

Unlike other Jewish holidays, *Shavuot* has no prescribed *mitzvot*, or religious duties, besides the traditional festival observances, which include attending special prayer services, eating holiday meals, and refraining from work. There are, however, several customs associated with *Shavuot*.

It is customary to adorn homes and synagogues with flowers and foliage for *Shavuot*. These greens serve as a reminder that *Shavuot* was first and foremost an agricultural harvest festival and that today, too, we are to feel indebted to God for our material blessings.

Prior to the reading of the *Torah* on the first day of *Shavuot*, we chant the *Akdamot*, a beautiful poem written in Aramaic in the eleventh century. *Akdamot*, meaning "introduction," prepares the congregation for the *Torah* reading of the Sinai revelation and for our own "reenactment" of the Jews' acceptance of *Torah* at Sinai. The poem glorifies God for creating the world and for choosing Israel as His special people. It is written in a double acrostic pattern with the initial letters of the Hebrew alphabet spelling out the words, "Meir [author of the *Akdamot*], son of Rabbi Isaac, may he grow in *Torah* and in good deeds. Amen. Be strong and have courage."

Jews traditionally eat dairy foods on the first day of *Shavuot*. Treats such as cheesecake and cheese blintzes are often featured on the menu. There are a number of reasons given for this. On the holiday in ancient times, a two-loaf bread offering was brought to the Temple. To commemorate this, Jews today eat two meals on *Shavuot* a dairy meal and, then after a short interruption, a traditional holiday meal.

In addition, with the giving of the *Torah*, Jews now became obligated to observe the kosher laws. Since the *Torah* was given on *Shabbat* (the Sabbath), no cattle could be slaughtered, nor could utensils be prepared as kosher, so on that day, the people ate dairy.

"YOUR WORD IS A LAMP FOR MY FEET, A LIGHT ON MY PATH."

—PSALM 119:105

THE HIGHEST GOAL

What are your goals? Maybe it's losing ten pounds this year, or exercising five hours each week. Maybe it's to cross off a few items on your "bucket list." Or maybe your goals are more financially oriented — to save something from every paycheck, or to pay off any debt by the end of the year.

But what about your spiritual goals?

For the Jew, studying the Bible is one of the loftiest spiritual pursuits we can undertake. Our love for God is linked with our love for His word. Each day we pray:

> "With an eternal love hast Thou loved Thy people, the house of Israel; *Torah*, commandments, good deeds, and laws hast Thou imparted to us. Therefore, O Lord our God, when we lie down and when we rise up, we will ponder Thy laws and rejoice in the words of the *Torah* and commandments. For they are our lives and the length of our days and upon them we will meditate day and night."

Study of the Bible orders our daily lives and gives us the focus and

DEVOTION

inspiration that we need each day. It is the *Torah* (which literally means "teachings") that brings solace, inner strength, and spiritual fulfillment to the Jew, in good times and in bad. It is the *Torah* that guides our path, shapes our character, and links us with God. It is the *Torah* that enables us to truly know God.

By immersing ourselves in the sacred act of Bible study, we can come to better understand both the content and source of that divine word. For this reason, Jewish education and the study of the *Torah* are two of the most important *mitzvoth*, or religious duties, in all of the Jewish faith.

Simply put, they are our highest goals for our spiritual lives.

Psalm 119, the longest Psalm and longest chapter in the Bible, is a praise song and tribute to God's word. It is a wonderful meditation on the beauty of God's word and how it helps us stay pure and grow in faith.

Why not make it your goal to read through and meditate on Psalm 119 in the coming days? Write down all the many ways that God's word is a lamp for your feet and a light on your path.

Going Deeper for Christians

For a Christian perspective on studying God's word, read these Scriptures:

- Matthew 7:24–27
- John 13:17
- Romans 2:13; 15:4
- James 1:22–25

ראֹשׁ הַשָּׁנָה

"The LORD said to Moses, 'Say to the Israelites: "On the first day of the seventh month you are to have a day of sabbath rest, a sacred assembly commemorated with trumpet blasts. Do no regular work, but present a food offering to the LORD."'"

— LEVITICUS 23:23-25 —

ROSH HASHANAH

the Jewish New Year

The New Year for most of us evokes images of parties, confetti, fireworks, and football. But for Jews, the New Year ushers in a time of intense introspection of our lives and our souls. *Rosh Hashanah* and *Yom Kippur*, which mark this period of time known as the High Holy Days, are the most widely observed of all Jewish holy days. Even those Jews who normally don't attend synagogue services will observe these days.

The High Holy Days are a time of reflection and change, judgment and restoration, mercy and compassion. It is a time marked by repentance, by a desire to "wash our slates clean" and begin life anew. We observe these holy days with rich traditions and beautiful liturgies that are shared with families and friends.

Jews believe that God responds a thousandfold to humankind's even slightest turn toward Him.

A Time to Repent

Rosh Hashanah, the Jewish New Year, literally means "head of the year." Jews point to Leviticus 23:23–25 as the biblical origins of *Rosh Hashanah*. In this passage, God instructs Moses, *"Say to the Israelites: 'On the first day of the seventh month you are to have a day of sabbath rest, a sacred assembly commemorated with trumpet blasts. Do no regular work, but present a food offering to the Lord.'"*

These instructions are among the many laws God handed down to the nation of Israel through Moses at Mount Sinai. This was toward the beginning of the Israelites' forty-year journey through the desert after God rescued them from slavery in Egypt. During this intense period in the Israelites' history, God solidified His special relationship with His chosen people by leading them with the pillars of smoke and fire, providing for their needs in miraculous ways, and giving them the set of instructions and laws that Jews still observe to this day.

It is the meaningful and historic relationship that Jews have long held with God that comes to our mind on this day — and helps set the somber tone. We desperately want to please God and obey His righteous commands, and yet we realize that we are human and fall short of His holy standards. During the High Holy Days we appeal to God, the Supreme Judge and Ruler of the Universe.

According to tradition, it is during this time that God determines "who shall live and who shall die" in the coming year. Jews believe that God judges the world on *Rosh Hashanah* and writes our fate in one of three books: one for those who were righteous during the year; one for those who were wicked; and one for those whose good and bad deeds balanced. Our fate for the year to come is sealed ten days later on *Yom Kippur*, the Day of Atonement and the holiest day on the Hebrew calendar. It is during the ten days between *Rosh Hashanah* and *Yom Kippur* that Jews believe we can change the course of our destiny by repenting, praying, and doing acts of charity.

Foundational to Judaism is the concept that people possess the freedom and capacity to atone for their sins and to transform their lives. Everyone has the power to gain reconciliation with both God and others. Just as God sought out Adam, Cain, and Jonah when they tried to flee from Him, so God seeks out all humankind, confronting us with our sins and hoping that we will repent.

Jews believe that God responds a thousandfold to humankind's even slightest turn toward Him. As it says in the words of the *Midrash*, "My children, give me an opening of repentance no bigger than the eye of a needle, and I will widen it into openings through which even wagons and carriages will pass through" (Song of Songs Rab. 5:2).

"DO I TAKE ANY PLEASURE IN THE DEATH OF THE WICKED? DECLARES THE SOVEREIGN LORD. RATHER, AM I NOT PLEASED WHEN THEY TURN FROM THEIR WAYS AND LIVE?"

—EZEKIEL 18:23

HAPPY NEW YEAR?

During *Rosh Hashanah*, the image that best illustrates the tenor and pervading mood is that of a guilty party standing before a judge, pleading for mercy. Only in this instance, the Judge is the Supreme Ruler of the Universe; the guilty party, ourselves. It's understandable then, isn't it, that we approach this day with trepidation, "fear and trembling."

Yet, we also temper this solemn mood with one of trust and hope in a God — a merciful and beneficent Father — who desires our repentance and is eager to grant forgiveness. The prophet Ezekiel confirms this image of a benevolent, forgiving Father. Indeed, he writes, *"But if a wicked person turns away from all the sins they have committed and keeps all my decrees and does what is just and right, that person will surely live; they will not die. . . . Do I take any pleasure in the death of the wicked? . . . Am I not pleased when they turn from their ways and live?"* (Ezekiel 18:21, 23).

We take comfort and refuge in a compassionate Father whose perfect love causes Him to show mercy to those who recognize their sin and turn back to Him. In the beautiful words of Psalm 103, *"As a father has compassion on his children, so the* Lord *has compassion on those who fear him; for he knows how we are formed, he remembers that we are dust"* (vv. 13–14).

In God's economy of time, it is never too late to start afresh, to change direction, to turn toward Him and seek forgiveness. We don't have to wait for New Year's Day to make a change. Your "new year" can begin today as you turn your heart and your face toward God and trust that He is waiting for you.

Josiah Hears the Book of Law, by Julius Schnorr von Carolsfeld

GOING DEEPER FOR CHRISTIANS

For a Christian perspective on God's compassion for sinners, read these Scriptures:

- Luke 15:3–7
- 2 Peter 3:8–10

True repentance involves a "change of heart" and a "change in action."

Turning to Good

A central theme during the High Holy Days is repentance, or *teshuvah*, literally meaning "returning to one's self." According to Jewish traditions, four conditions are necessary for repentance: regret for the past; desisting from sinful behavior; confession before God; and resolving not to sin in the future.

True repentance, therefore, involves not only a "change of heart," but a "change in action" as well — turning away from bad and turning toward good. In the words of the Psalmist, *"Turn from evil and do good; seek peace and pursue it"* (Psalm 34:14).

The last month of the Jewish calendar, *Elul*, is actually the most important one in the Jewish calendar because it serves as the preparation for the High Holy Days, *Rosh Hashanah* and *Yom Kippur*. During the month preceding *Rosh Hashanah*, Jews have an opportunity to step back and assess the previous year. It is a time to clarify our life goals, to come closer to God. It is a time of realizing purpose in life, rather than just going through the motions. It is a time when we look at ourselves critically and honestly, with the intention of improving. It's a time to turn toward ourselves and evaluate our lives.

The first four Hebrew letters of the word *Elul (aleph-lamed-vav-lamed)* are the first letters of the words *Ani l'dodi v'dodi lee — "I am my beloved's and my beloved is mine"* (Song of Solomon 6:3). These words epitomize God's relationship with His people. *Elul* is a time when God reaches out to His people, and we in return, respond to Him through acts of repentance.

During evening and morning prayer throughout *Elul*, the Jewish people recite Psalm 27, echoing King David's heart cry, *"One thing I ask from the LORD . . . that I may dwell in the house of the LORD all the days of my life."* It is a time for us to focus on the unifying force of God in our lives and to increase our connection to Him.

"THEREFORE TELL THE PEOPLE: THIS IS WHAT THE LORD ALMIGHTY SAYS: 'RETURN TO ME,' DECLARES THE LORD ALMIGHTY, 'AND I WILL RETURN TO YOU.'"

—ZECHARIAH 1:3

GOD'S RETURN POLICY

Rosh Hashanah is among the most widely observed of all the holy days for Jews. I often wonder whether synagogues experience such high numbers because these days mark an opportunity for all Jews to wash their slates clean and begin life anew. Who, at one time or another, hasn't truly desired an opportunity to do just that?

Rosh Hashanah offers us that chance through *teshuvah*, or repentance. This is a time when we can turn away from evil and return to God. While Jews and Christians differ on man's ability to "atone" — how to pay for those sins — we all agree on our need to repent. And we all rely on God's graciousness and His mercy as we turn from our sinful ways and turn toward Him for forgiveness.

So, during this holiest time of the year, God seeks us out and confronts us, hoping that we will repent and cease sinning. Recall the biblical accounts of men such as Adam, Cain, and Jonah when they tried to flee or hide from God. The LORD met them face to face, giving them no choice but to stand before Him and account for their actions, however reluctantly. This is a good thing, though, because we

DEVOTION

believe God responds a thousandfold to a man's slightest inclination toward repentance.

And that is good news, indeed, for Jews and Christians alike.

So as we engage in this time of soul-searching, I encourage you to participate in *teshuvah* and to return to God as He most graciously promises to return to you.

Cain Kills Abel, by Julius Schnorr von Carolsfeld

GOING DEEPER FOR CHRISTIANS

For a Christian perspective on repentance, read these Scriptures:

- Matthew 4:17
- Luke 5:31–32
- Acts 2:38–39

“Awake, O you sleepers, awake from your sleep! Search your deeds and turn in repentance.”

A Time to Wake Up

The quintessential symbol of *Rosh Hashanah* is the *shofar*, a curved ram’s horn that was used during biblical times to, among other purposes, signal when to break camp, call to arms, and usher in feast days and the Sabbath. During *Rosh Hashanah*, the *shofar* is sounded one hundred times on each of the two days. According to Jewish tradition, there are three distinct types of blasts that are sounded — a long, drawn-out sound (*tekiah*), a broken, plaintive sound (*shevarim*), and a series of sharp, wailing staccato sounds (*teruah*). The most important *mitzvah* (deed) to be obeyed during *Rosh Hashanah* is to hear the sounding of the *shofar*.

There are many explanations for the sounding of the *shofar:*

Symbol of revelation. The *shofar* figured prominently in the drama of the giving of the *Torah* at Mount Sinai. In Exodus 19, we read *“On the morning of the third day there was thunder and lightning, with a thick cloud over the mountain, and a very loud trumpet blast. Everyone in the camp trembled”* (v. 16), and, *“As the sound of the trumpet grew louder and louder, Moses spoke and the voice of God answered him”* (v. 19). The *shofar* is a reminder for Jews to recommit ourselves anew to living according to the *Torah*.

Symbol of God’s coronation. The sounding of the *shofar* is a reaffirmation of God's sovereignty and kingship over us. In the words of the Psalmist, *"with trumpets and the blast of the ram's horn — shout for joy before the LORD, the King"* (Psalm 98:6).

Symbol of the *akedah* (binding of Isaac). The story of Abraham and Isaac in Genesis 22, and Abraham's willingness to sacrifice his only son, is read on *Rosh Hashanah*. The ram, whose horn was caught in the bushes, was sacrificed in place of Isaac. The ram's horn became an eternal symbol of Abraham's and Isaac's trust in God, even in the face of death.

Symbol of humankind's need for repentance. Just as the *shofar* was used during biblical times as a call for the people to assemble or as a warning of impending danger, the *shofar* is sounded on *Rosh Hashanah* as a wake-up call. It is a clarion call to perform *teshuvah* (repentance) and for moral introspection. Maimonides, the great medieval Jewish philosopher, explained the *shofar* in the following manner: "Awake, O you sleepers, awake from your sleep! Search your deeds and turn in repentance."

Symbol of the messianic era. Finally, the *shofar* is sounded as a reminder of God's promise to bring the Messiah who will usher into the world an era of physical and spiritual peace. The prophet Isaiah wrote, *"And in that day a great trumpet will sound. Those who were perishing in Assyria and those who were exiled in Egypt will come and worship the LORD on the holy mountain in Jerusalem"* (Isaiah 27:13).

"WHEN A TRUMPET BLAST IS SOUNDED, THE TRIBES CAMPING ON THE EAST ARE TO SET OUT. AT THE SOUNDING OF A SECOND BLAST, THE CAMPS ON THE SOUTH ARE TO SET OUT. THE BLAST WILL BE THE SIGNAL FOR SETTING OUT."

—NUMBERS 10:5–6

GOD'S WAKE-UP CALL

Maybe it's a failing grade on a midterm exam, or a high cholesterol reading at the annual physical. Perhaps it's a negative assessment at the six-month job performance review. Whatever the situation, this unexpected and unwelcomed news often serves as a warning for us. Change is required unless we want to face more dire circumstances.

During *Rosh Hashanah*, the Jewish people get such a wake-up call — both literally and figuratively — through the sounding of the *shofar*.

In biblical times, the *shofar* was sounded as a call for the people to assemble or for the camp to move on, as well as a warning of impending disaster. Similarly, it is sounded on *Rosh Hashanah* to arouse us from our moral reverie, to call us to spiritual regeneration, and to alert us to the need to engage in repentance. It is our signal to search our deeds and mend our ways before the awesome Judge. It is our reminder of our need to confront our inner selves and ask, as God did with Adam, the existential question: *"Where are you?"* (Genesis 3:9).

We all could benefit from such a warning. Maybe it's not the

DEVOTION

plaintive, drawn-out sound of a ram's horn, but consider what you might use as a physical and tangible reminder to pause, take a spiritual assessment, and make necessary changes.

What will be *your* wake-up call? And what will you be waking up to? Where are *you*?

Adam and Eve Hide From God,
by Julius Schnorr von Carolsfeld

Going Deeper for Christians

For a Christian perspective on heeding God's call, read these Scriptures:

- 1 Corinthians 6:9–11
- Galatians 6:7–8
- Hebrews 2:1–4
- 1 John 4:4–6

We throw bread crumbs or stones into a body of running water as a symbol of casting off our sins.

A Time of Traditions

Many meaningful and beautiful customs are associated with *Rosh Hashanah*. White is the predominant color scheme during *Rosh Hashanah* and the Days of Awe. The skullcaps, Ark curtain, and *Torah* mantles are all white, signifying purity, holiness, and atonement for sin. White is also the color of the shrouds in which Jews are buried. It is a solemn reminder of the gravity of God's judgment and of the frailty of life.

Other customs associated with the Jewish new year are as follows.

***Tashlikh* ceremony** — On the first day of *Rosh Hashanah*, Jews perform a ceremony called the *Tashlikh*, a symbolic casting away of sins. We throw bread crumbs or stones into a running body of water, such as a river or stream, as a symbol of casting off sin into the water and starting life anew. This custom started in the fifteenth century, most likely based on the biblical account of the scapegoats.

While some rabbis at that time prohibited the ceremony, today it is widely accepted and widely viewed as symbolic of the freedom from sin that can be enjoyed when we repent and trust in God's miracle of forgiveness. As we cast crumbs into the water, the words of the prophet Micah are recited, *"You [God] will again have compassion on us; you will tread our sins underfoot and hurl all our iniquities into the depths of the sea"* (Micah 7:19).

Traditional greetings — During *Rosh Hashanah* people greet one another with the words *"le-shanah tovah tikatevu v'taychataymu,"* which means "May you be inscribed and sealed for a good year." This comes from the traditional imagery in which God sits in judgment on the Days of Awe, deciding the fate of every living thing. On *Rosh Hashanah*, He opens the three books — one for those who were righteous, one for those who were wicked, and one for those whose good and bad deeds balance.

Everyone's fate is inscribed in one of those three books — and that fate is sealed on *Yom Kippur.*

As it says in Proverbs 16:2, *"All a person's ways seem pure to them, but motives are weighed by the Lord."* According to Maimonides, we are to constantly regard both our own fate as well as the destiny of the entire world as balanced between acquittal and guilt. By committing even one additional sin, we effectively tilt the scales of our lives and of the world toward guilt and destruction.

But we can also swing the scales toward good and help bring about our own salvation as well as that of the world by performing one good deed.

Cast Your Sins Away

"You will again have compassion on us; you will tread our sins underfoot and hurl all our iniquities into the depths of the sea."

—Micah 7:19

Remember your school days when the final exam was over, the dismissal bell rang, and you experienced that glorious rush of freedom? In that moment, you were released from the tyranny of schedules and deadlines, from the demands of teachers. The promise of summer stretched endlessly before you.

For most of us, those days are but a distant memory. Now, the to-do lists, work assignments, and daily demands of life never seem to diminish. As soon as one task is completed, another takes its place. Add to this the burden of our mistakes, the guilt caused by errors in judgment — our sins, if you will — and life can quickly become onerous. We long for the seemingly easier, less complicated times of our youth.

But imagine an opportunity to cast those burdens away and enjoy that sense of freedom again. In a way, that is what Jews symbolically experience when we perform the *Tashlikh* ceremony on the first day of *Rosh Hashanah*. Through this action, we are, in essence, casting off our sins into the water and beginning life anew. It is symbolic of the freedom from sin we can enjoy when we repent and trust in God's miracle of forgiveness. In the words of the prophet

DEVOTION

Micah recited in the *Tashlikh* liturgy, *"Thou wilt cast all our sins into the depths of sea."*

What burdens are you carrying today? Take a moment to write them down on a piece of paper. Now "cast them" before God, trusting that He will not only forgive you, but He will also remove your sins from you. Take comfort in these words from the Psalmist: *"as far as the east is from the west, so far has he [God] removed our transgressions from us"* (Psalm 103:12).

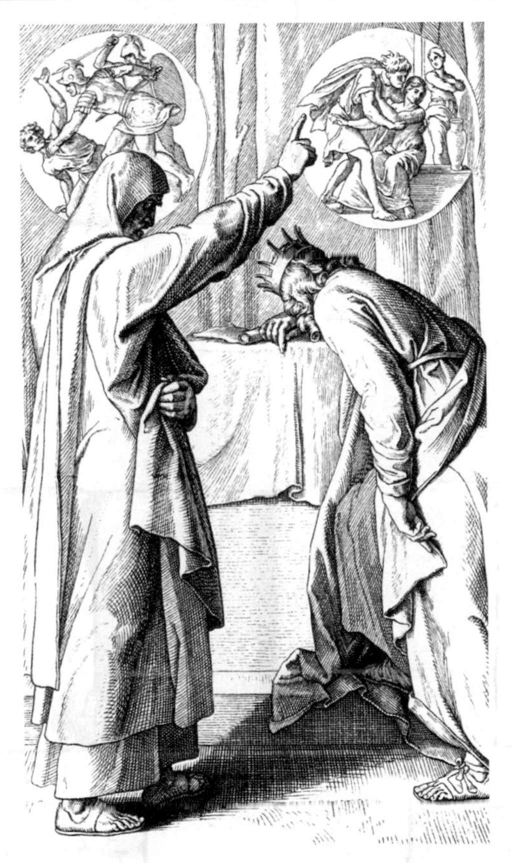

Nathan Rebukes David, by Julius Schnorr von Carolsfeld

GOING DEEPER FOR CHRISTIANS

For a Christian perspective on forgiveness, read these Scriptures:

- John 3:16
- Romans 6:20–23
- Hebrews 9:24–28

"May it be Thy will that we be blessed with a good, sweet year."

A Good and Sweet Year

Traditional foods are always an important part of any holiday observance, and *Rosh Hashanah* is no different. At *Rosh Hashanah*, we use a round *challah* (bread), symbolizing fullness and completion, and dip a piece of the bread into honey, which symbolizes the prayer for a sweet new year. That is followed by dipping an apple into honey and saying the blessing, "May it be Thy will that we be blessed with a good, sweet year." Jews ask for both because Judaism teaches that everything happens for the good. Even when circumstances look bad, they are actually "good." In asking that a year be "sweet," we also ask that these things be revealed as good — and therefore taste sweet!

The apple — Why the apple? The apple has quite significant meaning in Jewish tradition. In Song of Solomon, God's people are compared to an apple: *"Like an apple tree among the trees of the forest is my beloved [Israel] among the young men [the nations]"* (Song of Solomon 2:3). The *Midrash* teaches that the apple puts forth the nub of the fruit, even before the protecting leaves are fully sprouted. In a similar way, the Jewish people accepted the *Torah* and agreed to obey all God's commands even before knowing and understanding them all. Thus, the apple became a symbol for the moment of revelation at Mount Sinai.

The apple also serves to remind the Jewish people of their enslavement in Egypt and their deliverance from bondage. Again, the *Midrash* teaches that during that painful period of enslavement, the apple was served as a fruit representing the affection between husband and wife. It provided them with hope for the future and the determination to bring future generations into the world. The apple became the symbol of the Jewish home and family, of optimism for a brighter future, and of the tenacity and determination of the Jewish spirit.

Honey — Another favorite food during the High Holy Days is honey. During this time, honey is served with every major meal. In addition to being used for dipping bread and apples, honey is a key ingredient in baked goods served at this time, and is used in the preparation of foods such as glazed carrots and sweet desserts.

Having honey on the table during the High Holy Days is an ancient and universal Jewish custom. The obvious reason for the use of honey is the symbolism relating to the desire for a "sweet new year." But beyond that, honey represents one of the attributes of the Holy Land, described throughout the Hebrew Bible as a land *"flowing with milk and honey"* (Exodus 3:8). Honey on the table reminds Jews, no matter where they live, of their ancient homeland and of the Jewish attachment to its history and soil.

"THE LORD WILL SURELY COMFORT ZION AND WILL LOOK WITH COMPASSION ON ALL HER RUINS; HE WILL MAKE HER DESERTS LIKE EDEN, HER WASTELANDS LIKE THE GARDEN OF THE LORD. JOY AND GLADNESS WILL BE FOUND IN HER, THANKSGIVING AND THE SOUND OF SINGING."

—ISAIAH 51:3

A LAND OF MILK AND HONEY?

From the time God sent Moses to deliver His people from slavery in Egypt, the Israelites had been looking forward to the day they would arrive in the Promised Land, a land they had been told would be *"flowing with milk and honey."*

After leaving Egypt, the people of Israel wandered for forty years throughout the barren, arid desert. For forty years, they held tightly to God's promise of this beautiful, fruitful land. And when they finally arrived and entered the Promised Land, what did they find? More arid, barren land!

Can you imagine what they thought? Can you imagine their disappointment? *This* was the Promised Land?

But God had made a promise: If His people settled and worked the land, then it would be transformed from barren wilderness into gardens of Eden. But without the presence of His people, the land would refuse to bear fruit. And so it was — for nearly two thousand years after the Jews were expelled from the land!

But with the refounding of the modern State of Israel, the land has come to life again. It is, indeed, a land flowing with fruits and vegetables,

DEVOTION

forests and grain fields. It is a place of great beauty. God's promise to *"make her deserts like Eden"* (Isaiah 51:3) has been fulfilled.

So what does that mean for us? Perhaps you are in a desert right now. You are holding on to God's promise for His peace and restoration, but to be honest, you just don't see it. Each day looks and feels just like the ones preceding it. Where is God in the midst of your spiritual wilderness?

Hope can be found in the land of milk and honey. Just as God was faithful to make Israel's *"wastelands like the garden of the LORD,"* He will be faithful to His promises to you. Just as God surely comforted Zion, He will comfort you, and He will surely lead you to a place of *"joy and gladness."*

Moses Views the Promised Land,
by Julius Schnorr von Carolsfeld

GOING DEEPER FOR CHRISTIANS

For a Christian perspective on God's faithfulness in keeping His promises, read these Scriptures:

- Romans 15:8–9
- 2 Corinthians 1:20
- 2 Peter 1:3–5

"And all that have come into the world pass before you as a flock of sheep."

THE LITURGY AT *ROSH HASHANAH*

The liturgies associated with *Rosh Hashanah* are among the most beautiful and moving of the entire year. One of the most powerful, soul-stirring poems included in the liturgy is the *Unetaneh Tokef*. It purportedly was written by a rabbi from Mayence (Mainz) during the eleventh century, who underwent martyrdom during the first Crusade. It is a beautiful blend of ancient concepts and language from biblical and rabbinical sources.

Let us acclaim the majestic sanctity of this day, for it is awesome and mighty. Your kingdom is triumphantly proclaimed. Your throne is established in mercy, and you occupy it in truth. In truth, you are judge and prosecutor, knowing motives, giving evidence, writing, sealing, counting, measuring, remembering all, even things we have forgotten. You open the book of remembrances and it speaks for itself, for every person's signature is affixed to his deeds.

The great Shofar is sounded. A muted small voice is heard. The angels too are frightened, fear and trembling seize them, and they declare: "This is the day of judgment, of mustering the host on high!" In your sight not even they are exempt from judgment. And all that have come into the world pass before you as a flock of sheep. As a shepherd gathers his flock, making his sheep pass beneath his staff, even so do you make pass, count, and muster the souls of all the living. You determine the latter end of every creature and record their verdict. On Rosh Hashanah it is written down for them, on Yom Kippur it is sealed. How many shall leave [life] and how many shall be born, who shall live and who shall die, who shall attain his full span of life and who shall not, who shall perish by fire, and who by water, who by the sword and who by wild beasts, who by hunger and who by thirst, who by storm and who by plague, who shall have rest and who shall be restless, who shall find repose and who shall be wandering, who shall be free from sorrow and who shall be tormented, who shall be exalted and who shall be humbled, who shall be poor and who shall be rich. But Repentance, Prayer, and Good Deed can avert the severity of the decree.

For your renown is as your name; slow to anger, ready to be soothed. You do not desire the guilty one's death, but that he turn from his way and live. You wait for him up to the very day of his death; if he returns you accept him at once. Verily you are their Creator and you know their inner drives; they are but flesh and blood.

As to man, his origin is dust and his end is dust, at the risk of his life he earns his bread, he is like a broken vessel of clay, like withering grass, a fading flower, a passing shadow, a drifting cloud, a fleeting breath, scattering dust, a transient dream.

But you are King, God, living and enduring!

"HE TENDS HIS FLOCK LIKE A SHEPHERD: HE GATHERS THE LAMBS IN HIS ARMS AND CARRIES THEM CLOSE TO HIS HEART; HE GENTLY LEADS THOSE THAT HAVE YOUNG."

—ISAIAH 40:11

LIKE A SHEPHERD

One of the most basic human desires is to be known. We long for others to recognize us, to listen to us, and to accept us for who we are — flaws and faults included. Yet, how many of us can say we have truly and completely experienced that?

The *Unetaneh Tofek* is a celebration and acknowledgement of the One who not only fully knows us, but who also desires to have a relationship with us and draw us to Himself.

This prayer portrays God as a shepherd over His flock, counting and examining each sheep one by one as it passes under His rod. And while this time of judgment is approached by all — including the angels — with fear and trembling, the prayer affirms the central theme of the High Holy Days — "You do not desire the guilty one's death, but that he turn from his way and live."

And while the shepherd examines and judges each of sheep in his flock, the imagery also suggests a shepherd who deals with his flock gently and tenderly because he knows his flock. As the prayer continues, "Verily you are their Creator and you know their inner drives; they are but flesh and blood." The

DEVOTION

psalm writer affirms this thought: *"From heaven the LORD looks down and sees all mankind; from his dwelling place he watches all who live on earth — he who forms the hearts of all, who considers everything they do"* (Psalm 33:13–15).

Our Shepherd knows us. He created us, and He understands our frailties and our inclination toward sinfulness. Yet despite this, as we have seen expressed throughout the celebration of *Rosh Hashanah*, God accepts us and loves us. He is eager to extend His mercy and forgiveness to us as we turn toward Him and repent.

The invitation is open to you today. Come, your Shepherd is waiting and watching.

Jacob's Deal for Rachel,
by Julius Schnorr von Carolsfeld

GOING DEEPER FOR CHRISTIANS

For a Christian perspective on God as Shepherd, read these Scriptures:

- Mark 6:33–34
- John 10:11–18
- Hebrews 13:20–21
- 1 Peter 2:24–25

יוֹם כִּפּוּר

"This is to be a lasting ordinance for you: On the tenth day of the seventh month you must deny yourselves and not do any work — whether native-born or a foreigner residing among you — because on this day atonement will be made for you, to cleanse you. Then, before the LORD, *you will be clean from all your sins. It is a day of sabbath rest, and you must deny yourselves; it is a lasting ordinance."*

— LEVITICUS 16:29–31 —

YOM KIPPUR

the Sabbath of Sabbaths

The High Holy Days drama starts with *Rosh Hashanah*, the Jewish New Year. The following ten days are filled with prayer, repentance, and acts of charity. Now comes the final act, *Yom Kippur,* the last chance of the year to atone for sins and get right before God. It is the holiest day on the Jewish calendar or, as described in the *Torah,* the "Sabbath of Sabbaths."

At the end of *Yom Kippur,* Jews believe that God closes the Book of Life on our fate and judgment for the year to come. Our greeting to each other during this day, *"gemar chatimah tovah,"* or "May you be sealed [in God's Book of Life] for good," reflects our hope for the new year — that we have pleased God and received His forgiveness.

This is the day we address those areas where we are out of alignment and where we fall short.

A Time to Fast

As the Bible instructs, *Yom Kippur* is a day of self-denial. It's not about us today; it's about God and His desires for our lives. This is the day we address those areas where we are out of alignment and where we fall short.

During the 24-hour period of *Yom Kippur*, Jews fulfill the biblical commandment to deny ourselves by fasting from food and water, engaging in intense soul-searching, and praying for forgiveness. From the evening of the holiday until sundown the following day (except for the few hours when we go home to sleep), we are in the synagogue beseeching God for forgiveness and reflecting upon the course of our lives. It's like spring cleaning for the soul.

Yom Kippur is a day of inner purification and reconciliation with God and others. However, Judaism insists that repenting, fasting, and praying atone only for those sins between man and God. Those sins committed against our fellow man require that Jews seek forgiveness personally from those we have offended as well as from God. Therefore, this is a day of many humble and healing conversations.

To help us with this spiritual reckoning, Jews fast on *Yom Kippur*.

This physical act is meant to help us focus on spiritual matters. It is a reminder of the frailty of human existence and of the duty to act charitably toward the less fortunate. The inspiring, yet sobering, words of Isaiah 58 are read publicly in the synagogue on *Yom Kippur* to reveal the true meaning of the *Yom Kippur* fast:

> *"Is not this the kind of fasting I have chosen: to loose the chains of injustice and untie the cords of the yoke, to set the oppressed free and break every yoke? Is it not to share your food with the hungry and to provide the poor wanderer with shelter — when you see the naked, to clothe them, and not to turn away from your own flesh and blood?"*
> —Isaiah 58:6–7

"THIS IS TO BE A LASTING ORDINANCE FOR YOU: ON THE TENTH DAY OF THE SEVENTH MONTH YOU MUST DENY YOURSELVES AND NOT DO ANY WORK — WHETHER NATIVE-BORN OR A FOREIGNER RESIDING AMONG YOU."

—LEVITICUS 16:29

A TRUE FAST

What does it mean for you to deny yourself? Is it foregoing your favorite dessert? Or turning off the television one night a week to spend more time with your family or friends? Perhaps it's sacrificing that extra hour of sleep so you can spend time in God's word. Denying ourselves can be as minor as giving up that piece of chocolate cake or as significant as turning down a job promotion so we can be more involved in ministry.

Self-denial is a key element in the observance of *Yom Kippur*. In fact, God commands that we "must deny" ourselves during this time. Not only do we cease from all work on *Yom Kippur*, but we also honor God's command to deny ourselves by fasting, soul-searching, and praying.

Fasting is not to be seen as an end in itself, but rather as a prompt for us to focus on spiritual matters. For you see, we are also reminded during this time of the true meaning of the fast. The words of the prophet Isaiah, 58:6–7, are read during the *Yom Kippur* service to help us focus on that meaning.

DEVOTION

Fasting should be more than just denying ourselves food and water. We are called to take our fasting beyond our personal growth to acts of kindness and compassion, justice and charity. We are all called, Jews and Christians alike, to serve one another by seeking justice for the oppressed, feeding the hungry, clothing the needy, and sheltering the homeless. This is the *true* fast, the true meaning of denying ourselves and taking up the cause of those less fortunate than ourselves.

The True Fast - Giving Bread to the Hungry - Isaiah 58

And that is what truly pleases God.

GOING DEEPER FOR CHRISTIANS

For a Christian perspective on fasting, read these Scriptures:

- Matthew 6:16–18; 9:14–17 (see also Mark 2:18–22; Luke 5:33–39)
- Acts 13:1–3; 14:23

Since the beginning of creation, immersing oneself in water has been seen as the gateway to purity for God's people.

A Time to Purify

Besides fasting, a number of other Jewish customs and traditions are associated with *Yom Kippur*. For example, Jews immerse ourselves in a *mikvah*, or ritual bath, beforehand in order to fulfill the biblical command, *"They must purify themselves with the water on the third day and on the seventh day; then they will be clean"* (Numbers 19:12). The *mikvah* offers the individual, the community, and the nation of Israel the remarkable gift of purity and holiness.

It was on *Yom Kippur* that the High Priest was allowed entrance into the Holy of Holies, the innermost chamber of the Temple. This was the zenith of a day that involved a series of services and rituals — all of which were preceded by immersion in a *mikvah*.

Since the beginning of creation, immersing oneself in water has been seen as the gateway to purity for God's people. According to the *Midrash* (traditional Jewish literature), after being banished from Eden, Adam sat in a river that flowed from the garden. This was an integral part of his repentance process and of his attempt to return to his original perfection. Later, at the foot of Mount Sinai, all the people of the nation of Israel were commanded to prepare themselves for meeting God by immersing themselves in a *mikvah*.

The critical function of the *mikvah* was not to enhance physical hygiene as much as it was a spiritual exercise. Like many aspects of Jewish life that promote separation and distinction, the *mikvah* is the threshold separating the unholy from holy. Immersion in a *mikvah* signals a major change in status — more specifically an elevation in status. It symbolizes purification and regeneration, as well as new birth through repentance.

Sound familiar? The practice of *mikvah* is the origin of baptism for Christians. When John the Baptist stood on the Jordan River preaching baptism (which is the Greek word for "immersing") for all who repented of their sins, this would have been a familiar concept for his Jewish audience. In fact, when non-Jews converted to Judaism in biblical times and even today, they had to undergo a *mikvah* ritual as a sign of their passing from the worship of idols to the worship of the one true God.

"HE [THE HIGH PRIEST] SHALL BATHE HIMSELF WITH WATER IN THE SANCTUARY AREA AND PUT ON HIS REGULAR GARMENTS. THEN HE SHALL COME OUT AND SACRIFICE THE BURNT OFFERING FOR HIMSELF AND THE BURNT OFFERING FOR THE PEOPLE, TO MAKE ATONEMENT FOR HIMSELF AND FOR THE PEOPLE."

—LEVITICUS 16:24

COMING CLEAN

If you have ever worked in the garden pulling weeds during a hot summer day, you know how grimy a body can get — and you know how revitalizing it is to wash away all that dirt and grime with a refreshing shower. Once the dirt has been removed and you are completely clean, you feel like a new person, renewed and revitalized.

In a sense, this is the underlying principle of the priests who were commanded by God to wash themselves before entering the Tabernacle and preparing sacrifices for the people during the Day of Atonement. On one level, the priest was preparing himself spiritually for worship by bathing himself. Immersing himself in the water was a sign of purification and regeneration.

This purification ritual was also prescribed by priests to those who were deemed unclean, whether from an illness, being in contact with someone who was ill, or any number of things that the *Torah* deemed were unclean. The "unclean" person was washed, and therefore, made clean and presentable before God.

Before *Yom Kippur*, many observant Jews practice this tradition,

DEVOTION

immersing ourselves in a *mikvah* or "ritual bath." This physical act not only symbolizes our act of purifying ourselves before God, but also our "new birth" through repentance.

Most of us don't go a day or more without cleaning ourselves physically. It's an important part of preparing ourselves for our daily activities. But what about our need for spiritual cleansing? How can you "prepare" yourself to come before God, whether it's in a formal worship service or your quiet time with Him? Memorizing verses like Psalm 26:6–7, Psalm 51:1–2; 7, or Ezekiel 36:25 might be a good way to "cleanse" and revitalize yourself spiritually.

Preparing the Water of Separation

GOING DEEPER FOR CHRISTIANS

For a Christian perspective on baptism, read these Scriptures:

- Matthew 3:13–17 (see also Mark 1:9–11)
- Luke 3:21–22
- Matthew 28:18–20 (see also Mark 16:15–16)
- Romans 6:1–5
- Ephesians 4:4–6
- 1 Peter 3:18–22

We see Jonah's story as a reminder that we can never flee from God and His judgment.

A Tale of Caution

Though there are many fascinating themes in the book of Jonah, for Jews the book about the wayward prophet is primarily about repentance and redemption. This is why we read it every year at *Yom Kippur*. We see Jonah's story as a reminder that we can never flee from God and His judgment, and as an affirmation that He seeks our repentance and longs to forgive us and shower us with His love.

All the activities of *Yom Kippur* bring with us a heightened awareness of our fallen nature — of the punishment we deserve and our desperate need for God's mercy. And it is with this perspective that we hear the story of Jonah on *Yom Kippur*.

Who was Jonah? He was a reluctant prophet who ran from God's clear directive to go to Nineveh and preach His truth. He was a defiant believer who wanted mercy for himself, but not for the people of Nineveh, and admitted to his boat-mates that he worshipped *"the LORD, the God of heaven, who made the sea and the dry land"* (1:9) even as he was trying to flee from God in a wooden ship. He was a forgetful man who — even after he was miraculously saved from the seas, the storms, and the sea creature — had the audacity to get angry with the

God who rescued him.

And in all these unsavory qualities we find ourselves — sinful, broken, selfish, disobedient, and desperately in need of God's forgiveness. Biblical scholars disagree on who Jonah was, when the book was written, and who wrote it, creating ambiguity that makes it all the easier for us to identify with this cautionary tale.

The book of Jonah makes us painfully aware of our need for atonement and all the more grateful for a God who, as Jonah reminds us, is a *"gracious and compassionate God, slow to anger and abounding in love, a God who relents from sending calamity"* (4:2).

A Second Chance

"He prayed to the Lord, 'Isn't this what I said, Lord, when I was still at home? That is what I tried to forestall by fleeing to Tarshish. I knew that you are a gracious and compassionate God, slow to anger and abounding in love, a God who relents from sending calamity.'"

—Jonah 4:2

Who hasn't acted like Jonah at some time or another? As you'll remember, when Jonah was called by God, he ran the other way. When God asked Jonah to help others, especially those sinners in Nineveh, Jonah refused. In fact, throughout the four short chapters of this book, Jonah is primarily interested in one thing — himself.

Yet, despite Jonah's selfishness, his stubbornness, *and* his disobedience, God pursued him. God gave him another chance, and when Jonah blew that, God offered him yet one more opportunity to do the right thing and help others. (Is any of this sounding familiar?)

We read the story of Jonah on the afternoon of *Yom Kippur* because it is our last chance of the year to repent before God and to change the direction we've been headed in — much like Jonah. The book of Jonah is the story of last chances, not only for himself, but for the people of Nineveh as well. Repent — or else — is the message.

But through it all, we see a gracious God who is willing to forgive, who is gracious and compassionate to all who will turn toward Him. Even Jonah knew this!

DEVOTION

If you think you have run out of chances with God, think about Jonah. If you feel like you've been heading in the wrong direction, be encouraged by Jonah's story. It's never too late with God to change direction and to seek forgiveness from Him. We can never flee from God and His judgment, but it's also equally true that He is *"a gracious and compassionate God, slow to anger and abounding in love"* (Psalm 103:8).

Jonah Preaching to the Ninevites, by Gustave Doré

GOING DEEPER FOR CHRISTIANS

For a Christian perspective on God's forgiveness, read these Scriptures:

- Matthew 6:14–15; 18:21–35
- Luke 6:36–38
- Acts 2:37–39; 10:42–43
- Ephesians 1:6–8
- 1 John 1:8–10

This prayer encapsulates the Jewish historical experience and vision for the future.

A Time to Confess

On *Yom Kippur*, Jews attend synagogue, where the mood is one of solemnity and awe but also of hope. A spirit of holiness pervades the congregation as we stand before God during this final 24-hour period before the end of the year. All appeal to the eternal Judge for a merciful judgment.

The services on *Yom Kippur* morning and afternoon contain a number of unique features. Jews recite a series of confessionals for sins we may have committed during the course of the past year.

In another portion of the service, worshippers remember our ancestors who suffered martyrdom rather than abandon their faith in God. We also recite prayers of *Yizkor*, or "remembrance," for the souls of deceased members of our families.

Evening services commence with the recitation of the *Kol Nidrei* prayer, one of the most powerful and emotionally evocative in all of Jewish liturgy. *Kol Nidrei* is a plea for absolution from any and all unfulfilled vows a person may have made to God in the course of the year. One interpretation of the opening words of the *Kol Nidrei* says, "See, O Lord, what miserable sinners we are. We make promises to live better lives each year and yet always fall short of keeping them. Therefore, help us, O Lord, and pardon us for our shortcomings."

This prayer grew out of a strong tendency among Jews in ancient Israel to make vows to God. Rash vows to God made for whatever reason were to be taken and dealt with seriously, as evidenced from Deuteronomy 23:21: *"If you make a vow to the LORD your God, do not be slow to pay it, for the LORD your God will certainly demand it of you and you will be guilty of sin."*

The *Kol Nidrei* thus developed from the longing for a clear conscience on the part of those seeking reconciliation with God, and so became an integral and moving part of the *Yom Kippur* service.

At the opening of every *Yom Kippur* service, Jews feel an abundance of emotions as we listen to the sorrowful strains of the *Kol Nidrei* melody and recall our history of persecution and suffering. Both the words and the melody of the prayer end in a triumphant note of optimism, leading from despair to hope. This prayer encapsulates the Jewish historical experience and vision for the future.

"LORD, WHO MAY DWELL IN YOUR SACRED TENT? WHO MAY LIVE ON YOUR HOLY MOUNTAIN? THE ONE WHOSE WALK IS BLAMELESS, WHO DOES WHAT IS RIGHTEOUS, WHO SPEAKS THE TRUTH FROM THEIR HEART."

—PSALM 15:1–2

THE POWER OF WORDS

I'm sure most of us can remember that childhood retort when someone called us a nasty name on the playground: "Sticks and stones may break my bones, but words will never hurt me." As adults, I think we can all agree that sometimes that is not true at all. Words *can* and *do* hurt us.

Given the time, I am sure we could all remember a stinging comment from a boss about our work performance, a slight from a colleague, or a criticism from a parent that has stuck in our psyche long after the words were uttered. We all know that words are, in fact, very powerful, and how we use them actually reflects upon our relationship with God.

King David understood this. In Psalm 15, he posed the question, *"LORD, who may dwell in your sacred tent?"* In the next verse, David provides the answer: *"The one whose walk is blameless, who does what is righteous, who speaks truth from their heart."* Such a person, according to David, doesn't slander his neighbor, keeps her promises, and doesn't insult others.

DEVOTION

The Proverbs give much attention to our use of words. The godly person uses words that are helpful (10:32), bring healing (12:18), and offer encouragement (12:25). This person knows exactly the right thing to say at the right time (15:23). In contrast, the godless person uses words that are perverse (10:32), that are hurtful and destructive (11:9), and which crush the spirit (15:4). As Proverbs 12:18 says, *"The words of the reckless pierce like swords."*

King Solomon, by Gustave Doré

Our words can destroy, crush, and pierce. Or they can heal, encourage, and help. As people of faith, Jews and Christians alike, how we use our words should reflect the One we serve.

Who can dwell in God's sacred tent? The one who uses his or her words carefully, thoughtfully, truthfully, and with integrity.

GOING DEEPER FOR CHRISTIANS

For a Christian perspective on the power of words, read these Scriptures:

- Matthew 12:33–35
- Romans 10:8–10
- Ephesians 4:29
- James 3:1–12

God extends His love to us by responding a thousandfold to our turning from sin.

A Time to Repent

As mentioned previously, true repentance, according to Jewish tradition and teaching, involves turning away from evil and returning to God and to our true, pure selves. The rabbis insist that *teshuvah*, or repentance, is an act of will that we are capable of asserting — no matter how caught in sin we are.

Jewish teaching holds that man is never too ridden with sin that he cannot turn toward God and initiate his own moral regeneration and renewal. For while God created man with both evil and good inclinations, He also provided us with the antidote to the power of evil — the *Torah*. The more we read the story of God and His plan for our lives, the more His truths get planted in our hearts, the more capable we become of turning from our desires to His.

Teshuvah is also dependent on the notion that God does not desire *"the death of the wicked, but rather that they turn from their ways and live"* (Ezekiel 33:11). God is a merciful and compassionate Father, as well as a just Judge. Jewish teaching tells us that God created and governs the entire world through a combination of His attributes of mercy and justice.

When we consider God's justice, power, and holiness, we realize that our ability to initiate reconciliation and inner healing is itself a divine miracle and act of grace. God extends His love to us by responding a thousandfold to our turning from sin. This Jewish view of repentance was inspired by the prophets who declared, *"'Return to me,' declares the Lord Almighty, 'and I will return to you'"* (Zechariah 1:3).

God's ability and desire to forgive are amazing realities year-round, but Jews make a deliberate effort to celebrate and accept these wondrous gifts at *Yom Kippur*.

THE PERFECT PARENT

"AS A FATHER HAS COMPASSION ON HIS CHILDREN, SO THE LORD HAS COMPASSION ON THOSE WHO FEAR HIM."

—PSALM 103:13

Most parents would agree that when it comes to raising children, a balance of discipline and love is required. Without discipline, children grow up knowing no boundaries. Without love, children grow up scarred and wounded. In either situation, the children suffer the consequences.

We see this dual balance of love and discipline modeled by God, our Father and Perfect Parent. Throughout the High Holy Days, as we are called to repentance, we also see repeatedly in Scripture that God is waiting and willing to forgive us.

But that does not mean God governs the world and "raises" us with mercy alone. If He allowed *only* compassion to rule all His decisions, the world would not survive because it would be filled with rampant, unchecked sinfulness. But as we also see in Scripture, God is perfectly holy and perfectly just; He rules His people and the world with justice as well. Yet, He cannot rule the world with strict justice either, because no one could stand up before His scrutiny and judgment. Instead, God rules the world with both justice *and* compassion.

We see evidence of these characteristics in the names that God calls

DEVOTION

Himself in the Bible. *Elo-him*, or "God," refers to God's justice, while *Ado-nai*, "LORD," alludes to His mercy. Remember when God told Noah that He intended to bring a flood *"to put an end to all people"* (Genesis 6:13)? The name *Elo-him* was used. However, as the flooding began and Noah and his family were led safely into the ark, the name *Ado-nai* was used to show God's compassion because He had saved them from destruction. We look to God, as David did in Psalm 103, to have compassion on us just as *"a father has compassion on his children."*

Noah's Thanksgiving Sacrifice, by Julius Schnorr von Carolsfeld

The beauty of this spirit of repentance is the urgency and meaning that it gives to our lives, compelling us to live each day for Him — trusting Him, obeying Him, and appreciating His grace for all His children.

GOING DEEPER FOR CHRISTIANS

For a Christian perspective on God's compassion, read these Scriptures:

- Matthew 9:35–37
- Mark 6:30–44 (see also Matthew 14:13–21; Luke 9:10–17; John 6:1–15)
- Luke 15:11–32
- Ephesians 4:31–32
- Colossians 3:11–13

“The day is passing fast, and the sun is going home and setting, do let us enter your gates. Forgive us, pardon us, have mercy.”

A Time for Forgiveness

Another special service held during *Yom Kippur* is the *Avodah* service. During that service we recall how the High Priest in the ancient days entered the Holy of Holies to purge it of uncleanness and to pray for forgiveness for the House of Israel (see Leviticus 16).

This ritual was enacted in biblical times as the High Priest first made atonement for his own sin by making the appropriate sacrifices and then for the sins of his household. Finally, the High Priest would set aside two goats, and lots would be cast to choose one of the two to be the “scapegoat.” The High Priest slaughtered the one goat to atone for the sins of Israel and brought the blood into the Holy of Holies. Then the priest would lay both hands on the head of the other goat and confess the sins of Israel before sending the goat away to be lost in the desert.

The two goats, in effect, represented the two ways God dealt with the people’s sins: He forgave their sins through the sacrifice of the first goat, and He removed the guilt of their sins through the second goat that was sent into the wilderness.

Then, as nightfall approaches and *Yom Kippur* is about to end, Jews pray the *Neilah*, or “closing service.” The liturgy of this service describes the heavenly gates as closing, leaving man, the petitioner, with a last opportunity to plead his case before final judgment.

Part of the *Neilah* liturgy pleads: "Open unto us the gate at the gate's closing time, for the day is almost over. The day is passing fast, and the sun is going home and setting, do let us enter your gates. Forgive us, pardon us, have mercy."

The prayer service reaches its climax as the congregation declares the central Jewish affirmation, *"Hear, O Israel, the LORD our God the LORD is One. Blessed be His glorious kingdom forever and ever,"* and repeats seven times the phrase, "God is the LORD."

The service concludes with one blast of the *shofar*, or ram's horn. The congregation, trusting in God and confident of His favorable judgment, proclaims, "Next year in Jerusalem!" This proclamation reflects our love of the Holy Land as well as our desire that within the coming year Messiah will come and gather all his people to Israel with him — that next year we will be able to celebrate *Yom Kippur* with him. After this sentiment is sung in joyful song, the drama of the Day of Atonement has reached its finale. The High Holy Days have come to a close.

"LET THE WICKED FORSAKE THEIR WAYS AND THE UNRIGHTEOUS THEIR THOUGHTS. LET THEM TURN TO THE LORD, AND HE WILL HAVE MERCY ON THEM, AND TO OUR GOD, FOR HE WILL FREELY PARDON."
—ISAIAH 55:7

TRUE REPENTANCE

As we have mentioned before, repentance is at the heart of the Jewish High Holy Days. But what does *true* repentance look like? According to Jewish tradition, there are four components of repentance: feeling regret for past sins; stopping sinful behavior; confessing before God; and resolving not to sin in the future. As Psalm 34 entreats, we must *"turn from evil and do good."* A change of heart and acknowledgement of our sin must be accompanied by a change in our behavior.

We find a similar invitation to repent and *"turn from evil"* in the book of Isaiah. In chapter 55, the prophet Isaiah extends God's invitation to repentance and redemption. By looking at the verbs in verses 3–7, we get another glimpse into God's heart. First, we are invited to come to God (v. 3) and to listen to Him so *"that you may live."* Second, we are to seek God while He can be found and to call upon Him. There is a sense of urgency to our need to repent — this is not to say that God will move away from us, but rather our tendency is to move away from Him. Finally, we are urged to turn to God, to forsake our evil ways, for then God will have mercy on us and *"freely pardon"* us (v. 7).

What a beautiful — and encouraging — invitation. But it is up to us to

DEVOTION

accept that invitation and to act upon it. When we have truly repented, a burden is lifted from our hearts. Our soul is cleansed, and our inner turmoil caused by our sinfulness is replaced with spiritual tranquility and inner peace. We have tasted God's goodness, and we are rewarded by an even greater desire to pursue goodness and righteousness.

The Psalmist David: Repentance, by Julius Schnorr von Carolsfeld

And we will know we have achieved *true* repentance when we choose *not* to sin in circumstances where we might previously have sinned.

What a divine miracle, a profound mystery, and a true demonstration of grace! Give thanks to God today that His invitation is open to us, and as the Psalmist writes, *"The LORD is near to all who call on him, to all who call on him in truth"* (Psalm 145:18).

GOING DEEPER FOR CHRISTIANS

For a Christian perspective on repentance, read these Scriptures:

- Luke 13:2–5; 15:1–10; 17:1–4
- Acts 2:37–41; 3:18–20
- 2 Peter 3:8–10

סוּכּוֹת

"The Lord said to Moses, 'Say to the Israelites: "On the fifteenth day of the seventh month the Lord's Festival of Tabernacles begins, and it lasts for seven days."'"

— LEVITICUS 23:33-34 —

SUKKOT

the Time of Our Happiness

The festival of *Sukkot* is the most joyous of the Jewish calendar and one of the three biblically mandated feasts or celebrations. In contrast to the somber gravity of the High Holy Days, four days after the High Holy Days end, *Sukkot* ushers in an atmosphere of rejoicing, reflecting the biblical command to *"be joyful at your festival"* (Deuteronomy 16:14). In fact, *Sukkot* is known as "the time of our happiness."

As described in the book of Leviticus, *Sukkot* is a time for Jews to exult in God's bounty, specifically the plentiful harvest (the festival occurs in the fall) and God's overflowing generosity in rescuing the Israelites from slavery in Egypt and guiding them through the desert to the Promised Land. Ultimately, though, *Sukkot* is about trusting God and relying completely on our relationship with Him.

Sukkot reminds us that all our material and earthly possessions come from God, and that we are utterly dependent on Him.

Temporary Dwellings

During *Sukkot*, also called the Feast of Tabernacles or Festival of Booths, Jews are commanded to build *sukkot* — booths in which we "dwell" for the duration of the holiday. (The singular is "*sukkah*.") The little makeshift huts look somewhat funny dotting backyards here in America, but they are breathtakingly beautiful when seen clinging to seemingly every corner of Israeli apartment buildings in Jerusalem. For eight days (seven in Israel), Jews "dwell" in these huts — eating, socializing, and sometimes, even sleeping in them.

Meant to remind us of the shelters in which the Israelites lived during their sojourn in the desert, *sukkot* deliberately are built to be temporary, impermanent. They have no fixed walls and their roofs are made of palm fronds or bamboo mats, something loose so that we can see the stars while resting inside.

The biblical description of the Jews wandering in the desert tells us that *"by day the LORD went ahead of them in a pillar of cloud to guide them on their way and by night in a pillar of fire to give them light"* (Exodus 13:21). Jewish tradition usually refers to the cloud pillar as "the Clouds of Glory," referencing the divine presence and protection they evidenced and provided. This terminology hints at the deeper meaning of *Sukkot*: Ultimately our protection and sustenance comes from God, who deserves our complete trust in Him.

Our homes, our livelihoods, our health . . . we have an obligation to do all we can to provide and safeguard them, but ultimately, they come from Him. That truth would have been far clearer to the ancient Israelites wandering in the desert, led and shaded by clouds during the day, warmed, with light by fire at night, sustained by manna, sleeping in huts they pitched every night. Their utter dependence on God was self-evident; we, on the other hand, can delude ourselves by thinking that all we have —materially and otherwise — comes from our own efforts and skill.

Sukkot reminds us that *all* our material and earthly possessions come from God, and that we are utterly dependent on Him.

This truth, then, is the source of joy at *Sukkot*, indeed, "the time of our happiness." For what greater delight, what deeper pleasure can there be than the knowledge that God is with us at every moment? That He is the source of everything, and that we are His beloved children and servants? We dwell in booths to remind us of all this, and, in so doing, we spend time with our Most Beloved, dwelling with the Ineffable.

It's Only Temporary

"Live in temporary shelters for seven days: All native-born Israelites are to live in such shelters so your descendants will know that I had the Israelites live in temporary shelters when I brought them out of Egypt. I am the Lord your God."

—Leviticus 23:42–43

"It's only temporary." Has anyone ever said that to you when you are in the midst of a difficult situation? Maybe you're working with a difficult client, or you are recovering from an emergency surgery. Knowing that the situation is temporary — that an end is in sight — can help you endure.

At times, we also need to remember that our home here on earth is only temporary. Indeed, we are reminded throughout Scripture that we are but *"strangers"* and *"foreigners"* in this world. In His instructions to the people of Israel about the Year of the Jubilee, God told the people: *"The land must not be sold permanently, because the land is mine and you reside in my land as foreigners and strangers"* (Leviticus 25:23). And in his prayer for God's mercy, David acknowledged, *"I dwell with you as a foreigner, a stranger, as all my ancestors were"* (Psalm 39:12).

In Jewish tradition, we have a very real and tangible way of remembering this basic principle. *Sukkot*, or the Feast of the Tabernacles, not only marked a time of thanksgiving for God's provision, but it also commemorated the Jews' deliverance from bondage in Egypt and their

DEVOTION

subsequent wandering in the desert for forty years without a permanent place to call "home."

The booths and the *Sukkot* festival are great reminders to us to rejoice in God's constant protection of and provision for us. But it also reminds us that our homes are temporary dwellings and that life is fleeting. Our permanent home with God awaits us.

We find this expressed beautifully in the Christian New Testament book of Hebrews, describing the Jewish patriarchs of ancestors, Abraham, Isaac, and Jacob as: *"All these people were still living by faith when they died. They did not receive the things promised; they only saw them and welcomed them from a distance, admitting that they were foreigners and strangers on earth"* (Hebrews 11:13).

Next time you are discouraged by your circumstances and your current struggles, remember these problems are only temporary.

GOING DEEPER FOR CHRISTIANS

For a Christian perspective on the fleeting nature of life, read these Scriptures:

- Luke 12:16–20
- 2 Corinthians 4:16–18
- James 4:13–15

"The Four Species" are bound together and waved in all directions to emphasize that God is everywhere...

CELEBRATING OUR CREATOR

One of the key elements of *Sukkot* is known as "The Four Species," as described in Leviticus: *"On the first day you are to take branches from luxuriant trees — from palms, willows and other leafy trees — and rejoice before the LORD your God for seven days"* (23:40). This is a ritual in which the branches of an *etrog* (or citron, resembling a lemon) and the branches of three trees (the willow, myrtle, and *lulav*, or date palm) are bound together and waved in all directions to emphasize that God is everywhere and all our blessings are from Him.

As to the meaning of the Four Species, there are a variety of opinions. Some Jewish scholars say these elements refer to four parts of the human body — the lips, heart, eyes, and backbone — all of which praise God together as we say of Him, *"Who is like you, LORD?"* (Psalm 35:10).

Other scholars teach that the Four Species refer to four kinds of people: the *etrog* stands for people who read the *Torah*, and do good; the date palm stands for those who read the *Torah*, but do not do good; the myrtle represents people who do not read the *Torah*, but do good; and the willow stands for people who neither read the *Torah* nor do good.

Yet other religious leaders suggest these four plants remind Jews that people are also different yet must come together for a healthy society to function.

On the *Shabbat*, or Sabbath, that falls during the week of *Sukkot* or on the following *Shabbat*, the book of Ecclesiastes is read during the morning synagogue services. The book's emphasis on the fleeting nature of life echoes the theme of *Sukkot*, and its emphasis on death reflects the time of the year in which *Sukkot* happens (autumn). The closing sentences reinforce the idea that adherence to God and His *Torah* are the only worthwhile pursuits: *"Now all has been heard; here is the conclusion of the matter: Fear God and keep his commandments, for this is the duty of all mankind. For God will bring every deed into judgment, including every hidden thing, whether it is good or evil"* (Ecclesiastes 12:13–14).

In Good Times and in Bad

"For in the day of trouble he will keep me safe in his dwelling; he will hide me in the shelter of his sacred tent and set me high upon a rock."
—Psalm 27:5

When do you find your prayer life most active? During difficult times, or when life seems to be going smoothly? If we are honest, we are on our knees before God more often when we're struggling. God and His promises of protection and guidance are more relevant to our lives when we're feeling vulnerable or needy. But when everything is going well and we seem to be in control of our situation, we sometimes forget about Him.

God warned the Israelites about this in Deuteronomy 28, when He outlined the blessings for obedience that the people would enjoy — and the curses, if they did not obey Him. God specifically addressed what would happen if the people forgot Him during times of prosperity: *"Because you did not serve the Lord your God joyfully and gladly in the time of prosperity, therefore in hunger and thirst, in nakedness and dire poverty, you will serve the enemies the Lord sends against you"* (Deuteronomy 28:47–48).

Jews are reminded of our dependence on God in good times and bad during *Sukkot* when we willingly and obediently leave the comforts

DEVOTION

of our homes to live in temporary booths. By exposing ourselves to the elements, we put ourselves in a place where we realize that true security and shelter are found only as we remain in God's will and under His care and guidance.

During *Sukkot*, we are reminded of the transitory nature of our material possessions and the true vulnerability of human existence. By following these practices, we test our willingness, albeit in a small way, to sacrifice our comfort and convenience for the sake of simple obedience to God. Ultimately, we learn that no matter what our circumstances, in good times and in bad, we must remember the One who provides our material blessings.

What is your situation today? Are you enjoying good health and prosperity? Are you struggling, or in need of some encouragement? Whatever you are experiencing right now, God is there. All we need to do is *"worship the LORD with gladness"* (Psalm 100:2) and remember that true joy is rooted in our recognition of our dependence — at all times — on a loving, sovereign God.

GOING DEEPER FOR CHRISTIANS

For a Christian perspective on dependence on God, read these Scriptures:

- 2 Corinthians 1:8–10; 12:8–10
- Philippians 4:11–13

Jews pray on *Sukkot*, not only for our own welfare, but for that of the entire world.

A Time for Hospitality

One of the beautiful traditions associated with *Sukkot* is *ushpizin* (Aramaic for "guests"), inviting guests into our *sukkah* to partake in the celebration. Jews are commanded to practice hospitality on *Sukkot* by inviting others to join in the feast, especially those who are in need. Traditionally it was customary to have at least one poor person at a *Sukkot* meal, though in modern times many Jews donate funds to a charitable organization instead.

During the holiday, many Jews recite the *ushpizin* prayer, which includes welcoming the seven "exalted guests" into the *sukkah*. These guests represent the seven shepherds of Israel: Abraham, Isaac, Jacob, Moses, Aaron, Joseph, and David. According to Jewish tradition, each night a different guest enters the *sukkah* and offers a unique lesson from his life story. Jewish tradition holds that the *ushpizin* refuse to enter a *sukkah* where the poor are not welcome.

In addition to serving as a reminder of our duty to those less fortunate, each of these forefathers of faith also represents uprootedness: Abraham left his homeland for the land God promised to show him (Genesis 12:1); during a famine, Isaac went to Gerar (Genesis 26:1); when his brother Esau was angry with him, Jacob fled to his Uncle Laban's house (Genesis 28:2); Joseph was sold by his brothers to traveling merchants, who took him to a life of slavery in Egypt (Genesis 37:23–36); Moses and Aaron wandered in the Sinai Desert for forty years (Numbers 14:34); and David hid from Saul in the wilderness (1 Samuel 21, 24).

Even in their wanderings, each of these men contributed to the world through a godly trait: loving-kindness, strength, splendor, glory, holiness, eternity, and sovereignty. As Jews enter into voluntary uprootedness in their *sukkah*, we are inspired to experience these blessings and benefits.

Sukkot is also a time of universal blessings. It is considered the one festival that all people will be expected to observe in the messianic era. As we read on the first day of *Sukkot*, *"Then the survivors from all the nations that have attacked Jerusalem will go up year after year to worship the King, the Lord Almighty, and to celebrate the Festival of Tabernacles"* (Zechariah 14:16). For this reason, Jews pray on *Sukkot*, not only for our own welfare, but for that of the entire world.

"THE LORD WILL BE KING OVER THE WHOLE EARTH. ON THAT DAY THERE WILL BE ONE LORD, AND HIS NAME THE ONLY NAME."

—ZECHARIAH 14:9

BUILDING BRIDGES

Leaving our "comfort zone" and reaching out to someone (or a group of people) unlike ourselves is not something most of us readily embrace. It stands to reason that we are most comfortable with people who share our values and beliefs. Hence the name "comfort zone"!

But did you know that on *Sukkot*, Jews are *commanded* to reach out to those different from ourselves?

After the destruction of the First Temple and the exile of the Jewish people to Babylon, the celebration of *Sukkot* took on additional meaning. Not only were the temporary booths a reminder of the transitory nature of our earthly home and possessions, but they also came to represent the frailty and impermanence of Jewish life in the *diaspora* (those living outside the land of Israel).

For the Jew, the *sukkot* (or booths) became symbols of our longing for our ancient homeland and for the arrival of Messiah, when the entire world will be redeemed and brought together. So on *Sukkot*, we pray for that time to come: "Spread over us your tabernacle [*sukkah*] of peace. Blessed are thou O Lord, who spreads the tabernacle of peace

DEVOTION

over us and over all His people, Israel, and over Jerusalem."

The universal and messianic character of the holiday was affirmed by Zechariah in the prophetic portion of Scripture that is read on *Sukkot*: *"The LORD will be king over the whole earth. On that day there will be one LORD, and his name the only name"* (Zechariah 14:9).

For this reason, Jews are duty-bound during *Sukkot* to strengthen our link with others. Not only are we to leave the comfort of our homes to live in temporary shelters, we are also to leave our comfort zones and break out of the barriers that separate us from our neighbors. We are commanded to reach out and help build bridges of understanding.

That has been a goal and vision of the *International Fellowship of Christians and Jews* from its beginning. And we hope that this is a goal of yours as well. Consider what bridges you can help build with your neighbors and how you can contribute to understanding, particularly between our two faith communities.

GOING DEEPER FOR CHRISTIANS

For a Christian perspective on unity, read these Scriptures:

- John 17:23
- Romans 12:4–5
- 1 Corinthians 12:12–13
- Ephesians 2:16–18; 4:3–6

> The words "thank you" are expressing not only joy and happiness, but also an acknowledgment that these good things came from an outside source…

A Time for Thanksgiving

Though *Sukkot* now has rich spiritual meaning, it was actually agricultural in origin. This is reflected in the biblical name, the Feast of Ingathering. Originally the holiday was a day of thanksgiving for the fruit harvest, which ended around the time *Sukkot* is celebrated, and for God's provision through nature in the year that had just passed.

Throughout biblical history, this feast was one of the most important on the Jewish calendar, and because of that, many important ceremonies were held on this day. For example, in Deuteronomy 31:10–11, Moses commanded the Israelites to gather for a reading of the law during *Sukkot* every seventh year. King Solomon dedicated the First Temple in Jerusalem on *Sukkot* (see 1 Kings 8 and 2 Chronicles 7:1–10). And it was on *Sukkot* that the Israelites resumed their burnt offerings to God in Jerusalem following their return from exile in Babylon (Ezra 3:2–4).

For Jewish people, Thanksgiving Day is eclipsed by the biblical festival of *Sukkot*. As we build the *sukkah* structures on this day, we are reminded of God's past provisions and protection, as well as how dependent we still are on Him for our every need. By dwelling in an exposed, insecure hut, we are reminded that true security comes from being sheltered under God's protective wings.

From that knowledge springs forth gratitude—the same gratitude expressed for the harvest, for God's presence with the Israelites those many years ago. This is a day of joy and thanksgiving, and it is speculated that the American holiday of Thanksgiving has its origins in *Sukkot*. The time of year, the festive meal, and the heart of gratitude associated with Thanksgiving all point to this possibility.

While *Sukkot* is a time of thanksgiving and joy, it's also a time of humility. Thus, it mirrors the true nature of thanksgiving — because anyone who utters the words "thank you" is expressing not only joy and happiness, but also an acknowledgment that these good things came from an outside source, from the one being thanked. As people of faith, we regularly offer our thanks as an act of obedience, in words of worship, and as a declaration of utter dependence on our God.

"COME, LET US SING FOR JOY TO THE LORD; LET US SHOUT ALOUD TO THE ROCK OF OUR SALVATION. LET US COME BEFORE HIM WITH THANKSGIVING AND EXTOL HIM WITH MUSIC AND SONG."
—PSALM 95:1–2

CULTIVATING A GRATEFUL HEART

How do you tell God thank you? Do you do so privately during your quiet time with Him? Or maybe you write it down in your journal? Maybe it's just a fleeting thought, a whispered thanks, as you arrive safely home from a long journey, or as you witness the beauty of the setting sun.

The writer of Psalm 95 encourages us to tell God thanks in quite a different way. He invites us to *"sing for joy,"* to *"shout aloud,"* to come before God with thanksgiving on our lips, and to worship Him with music and song. According to the psalm writer, our hearts should be so brimming with gratitude to God for all that He has done that we can't help but bubble over with joy and shout out our thanks.

Is that how it is with you?

English author Gladys Bronwyn Stern once wrote that silent gratitude is of use to no one. And inspirational writer William Arthur Ward put it this way, "Feeling gratitude and not expressing it is like wrapping a present and not giving it." Expressing our thankfulness is meant to be shared with others, aloud. We need to tell the object of our gratitude what we're feeling, not just think about it. Not only is the recipient of gratitude blessed when we say "thank you," but

DEVOTION

we also are lifted up when we see the effects our words have on others and when we focus on the good things in our lives.

When we consider giving thanks as a gift to be given, as words to be shouted, as a song to sing in joy, it helps us to cultivate that attitude in our hearts. It is more than just an automatic response; giving thanks becomes a lifestyle that can inspire and encourage others.

The Psalmist David: Praise and Thanks, by Julius Schnorr von Carolsfeld

Rabbi Abraham Joshua Heschel, a great Jewish theologian, once said that gratitude is the only response that can sustain us through life's ups and downs. He summed up the necessity for giving thanks to God in this way: "It is gratefulness which makes the soul great."

As people of God, let's cultivate in our hearts an attitude and practice of gratitude every day so that our souls might be great and that we are a blessing to others.

GOING DEEPER FOR CHRISTIANS

For a Christian perspective on gratitude, read these Scriptures:

- Ephesians 5:19–20
- Colossians 3:15–17
- 1 Thessalonians 5:18

...learning and studying God's word never ends—it is a lifelong process because there is always more to understand.

Rejoicing in God's Book

Everybody loves a party, especially when we have a reason to celebrate—the birth of a child, a marriage, a graduation or job promotion, a special holiday or birthday. But have you ever celebrated reading through the Bible?

Every year, following the celebration of *Sukkot*, Jews celebrate *Simchat Torah*, which literally means "rejoicing in the *Torah*." It is a celebration of the completion of reading through the *Torah* over the previous year. You see, every Sabbath in synagogues around the world, Jews participate in public readings of the *Torah*, which comprises the first five books of the Bible. We begin with Genesis, chapter one, and finish with Deuteronomy's closing words. When the annual cycle of readings is completed, it's time to celebrate! And then we begin the annual cycle all over again.

And, indeed, it is a joyous celebration. All the *Torah* scrolls are taken out of the Ark and carried around the sanctuary seven times. There's singing and dancing, and everyone is involved, from our eldest member to our children, who lead the procession.

During this celebration, as many people as possible are given the honor of reciting a blessing over the *Torah* readings; in fact, even children are called for a blessing on *Simchat Torah*. In addition, as many people as possible are given the honor of carrying a *Torah* scroll in these processions. Children do not carry the scrolls (they are much too heavy!), but often follow the procession around the synagogue, sometimes carrying small toy *Torahs* (stuffed plush toys or paper scrolls). This is also a time when many synagogues hold confirmation ceremonies, or ceremonies marking the beginning of a child's Jewish education.

Simchat Torah not only is a demonstration of love of God's word and our gratefulness to God for giving us the gift of the Bible, but it also is a reminder for us that learning and studying God's word never ends—it is a lifelong process because there is always more to understand. In fact, the Hebrew term for a great *Torah* scholar is *talmid chakham*, which means "wise student."

"OH, HOW I LOVE YOUR LAW! I MEDITATE ON IT ALL DAY LONG. YOUR COMMANDS ARE ALWAYS WITH ME AND MAKE ME WISER THAN MY ENEMIES."

—PSALM 119:97–98

GOING DEEPER FOR CHRISTIANS

For a Christian perspective on obeying God's word, read these Scriptures:

- Luke 8:21; 11:27–28
- John 14:15, 23–24
- 1 John 2:4–6; 5:2–3

PEOPLE OF THE BOOK

Did you know that Jews, particularly Orthodox Jews, are known as the "people of the Book"?

That reputation has been earned largely because of our long-standing belief that the Bible is eternally valid and utterly authoritative. We believe, like many of our Christian brothers and sisters, that the Bible is the actual embodiment of God's word. We believe it was divinely transmitted and the primary source of God Himself.

Further, we believe that the word of God is complete. Everything needed for life and our spiritual growth can be derived from it. Psalm 19:8 instructs, *"The precepts of the LORD are right, giving joy to the heart. The commands of the LORD are radiant, giving light to the eyes."* God's word literally gives us the ability to see—His will, His laws, and His ways.

Still, we sometimes allow excuses to keep us from studying God's word. We don't have enough time to fit it in, or we don't know how to get started. Or we fear we won't be able to understand everything we read. But as God told the people of Israel, *"Now what I am commanding you today is not too difficult for you or beyond your reach. . . . No, the word is very near you; it is in your mouth and in your heart so you may obey it"* (Deuteronomy 30:11, 14).

As "people of the Book," Jews and Christians alike, that is good news for us! God's word is near to us in our hearts and our minds. All we need to do is obey.